Learning Made Easy

SPELLING

Made Easy

pil

Publications International, Ltd.

Lynne Blanton, Ph.D., is a writer and editor with Creative Services Associates, Inc., a publisher of educational materials for over 15 years. She has served as editor for both Rand McNally and Riverside Publishing Company and has a B.A. in English and History from Birmingham-Southern College and a Ph.D. in Communications from the University of Illinois.

Flora Foss is a writer and editor with Creative Services Associates, Inc. She has taught language arts and science to middle school students, literature and writing to junior college students, and poetry writing to students of all ages. She received a B.S. in Education in Biology and an M.A. in Literature from Northern Illinois University in DeKalb, Illinois.

Consultant:
Dorothy F. King, Ed.D., is a consultant in language and literacy and has served as Chair for the National Council of Teachers of English Commission on Curriculum.

Illustrations by Rémy Simard.

Cover illustration by Garry Colby.

Acknowledgments:
Excerpt on page 4 from WINNIE-THE-POOH by A. A. Milne, illustrated by E. H. Shepard, copyright © 1926 by E. P. Dutton, renewed 1954 by A. A. Milne. Used by permission of Dutton Children's Books, a division of Penguin Young Readers Group, a member of Penguin Group (USA) Inc., 345 Hudson St., New York, NY 10014. All rights reserved.

Louis Weber, CEO
Publications International, Ltd.
7373 North Cicero Avenue
Lincolnwood, Illinois 60712

Permission is never granted for commercial purposes.

Manufactured in China.

8 7 6 5 4 3 2 1

ISBN: 0-7853-8845-1

Contents

Why Spell Well?

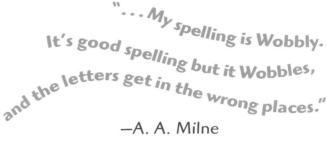

". . . My spelling is Wobbly. It's good spelling but it Wobbles, and the letters get in the wrong places."

—A. A. Milne
Winnie-the-Pooh

Spelling starts when you first learn to write—you put letters in a certain order that makes a certain word. What happens if you put the letters in the wrong odrer (order), leve (leave) a letter out, or substitute a wrong lettur (letter)? The word may become hard to recognize. To help people understand what you write, you must learn to spell.

Spelling Strategies

A large part of spelling is based on **patterns.** Certain letter patterns usually spell certain sounds. Learning these letter/sound relationships will help you spell a lot of words correctly. Of course, as you already know and as this book will demonstrate, there are many, many exceptions to the standard spelling rules. What can you do to help you find your way through these exceptions?

Adopt a Strategy

Follow these steps when learning to spell a word or when you're having trouble spelling a word.

1. Look at the word.
2. Say the word.
3. Spell the word.
4. Write the word.
5. Check the word.

You can also use **word structure** to help you spell. Use what you learn about the way words are structured to help you spell words with prefixes, suffixes, and endings. This strategy is also helpful for spelling compound words (*doghouse*), contractions (*couldn't*), and possessives (*grandmother's*). You can figure out how to spell some big words by breaking them into smaller parts based on their structure.

Spelling Helpers

Always remember that you have a really good friend that can help you spell: your dictionary. When you do not know how to spell a word or when you are unsure if you are spelling a word correctly, look up the word in a dictionary. It's a good idea to keep one conveniently within reach as you work on your homework.

Another very handy tool is the spell check feature on your computer. Spell checking works great for double-checking your work, but don't rely on it to catch all of your spelling miss takes. (Whoops! Did you notice the mistake in the previous sentence? Spell check didn't!) Because *miss* and *takes* are both perfectly good words, spell check didn't realize the sentence should have said *mistakes*.

Keep It Clean

The "cleaner" your writing is (that is, the fewer mistakes and misspellings there are), the easier it will be for someone to read. Misspellings distract people from what you're really trying to say, because instead of concentrating on what the words mean, they must stop and figure out what the words are.

Cn y cm
t m hs
ftr schl?
W cn lstn t
CDs r
wtch mvs.

Whatever you write—from a message for a friend to a book report—you want people to understand what you are writing. Spelling the words correctly will keep their attention fixed on your ideas, not on your mistakes. Use the easy lessons and fun quizzes in this book to help you develop your spelling skills. And have fun learning to be a super speller!

Consonants
The Skeleton of a Word

Words in English usually have both vowels and consonants. Let's look at the letters in our alphabet called consonants. Like bones that hold a body together, consonants are what hold words together.

Start with the Skeleton

Every word consists of one or more sounds. All of the letters in the alphabet help create these sounds, but consonants are what hold a word together, just as the bones of your skeleton hold your body together. The alphabet has 21 consonants (**b, c, d, f, g, h, j, k, l, m, n, p, q, r, s, t, v, w, x, y, z**). Sometimes **w** spells a vowel; sometimes **y** is a vowel.

If you listen carefully to the consonant sounds you hear in a word, you're on your way to figuring out how to spell the word. What sounds do the letters in the sign above spell? That's right! *Consonant.* Say it out loud.

To practice consonant sounds, try playing this game with a friend. Take turns writing messages to each other using only the consonants in words. See how well you can each read what the other writes. (You may also want to use this "shorthand" when making lists or notes for yourself.)

Cn y cm t m hs ftr schl? W cn lstn t CDs r wtch mvs.

Can you come to my house after school? We can listen to CDs or watch movies.

POP QUIZ

LETTER RIDDLE

Fill in the beginning consonants to figure out the riddle and its answer.

If it __akes __ive __eople one __ay to __ig up a __ield, __ow __ong __ill it __ake __en __eople to __ig up the __ame __ield?

Answer: __o __ime at all! The __ield __as already __een __ug up.

Answers on page 13.

Head Start: Consonants at the Beginnings of Words

Most English words begin and end with consonant sounds and letters. Many words begin with a single consonant sound spelled by a single consonant letter.

ball	lamp	ten
dog	man	van
fan	net	wing
hat	pig	yo-yo
jet	ring	zebra
king	sun	

EXCEPTIONS

Hold it! What about the consonants **c, g, q,** and **x?** Why are they missing from the beginning consonant list? You guessed it! They are different from the other consonants. The letters **c** and **g** can spell more than one sound, the letter **q** always needs help, and the letter **x** almost never appears at the start of a word.

"C" WHAT I MEAN? ~~~~ The sound of **c** in *cat* is called a hard **c,** and the sound of **c** in *cent* is called a soft **c.** The hard **c** sound is also sometimes spelled by the letter **k,** as in *keep* and *kiss.* The soft **c** sound is the same as the **s** sound spelled by the letter **s:** *same, sit.* It is usually pronounced as an **s** sound when it's followed by the letter **e, i,** or **y:** *center, city, cycle.*

hard c	soft c
cat	cent

"G," THIS IS FUN! ~~~~ The sound of **g** in *goose* is called a hard **g.** The sound of **g** in *giraffe* is a soft **g.** The letter **g** almost always spells the hard **g** sound. But the soft **g** sound is the same as the **j** sound spelled by the letter **j:** *jar, jump.* Like the letter **c,** the letter **g** often spells its soft sound when the letter **e, i,** or **y** follows the **g:** *germ, giant, gym.*

hard g	soft g
goose	giraffe

Q: May I Help You? ~~~~ Q always needs help. In English words, **q** is always followed by the letter **u.** Together they spell the beginning sound in words such as *queen, quick,* and *quarter.* You will almost never see the letter **q** without a **u** immediately following. This is an important spelling tip to remember!

X Marks the Spot ~~~~ Very few words begin with **x,** but when **x** does appear at the beginning of words, it usually sounds like its name (*X ray*). In a few words, however, such as *xylophone,* **x** is pronounced as the **z** sound. Because **x** doesn't spell a beginning sound of its own, you'll find it at the start of words quite infrequently. It usually spells the **z** sound and, even then, only in a very few unusual words.

Busy bugs bathe in bubbly bathtubs.

Silly Sentences and Similes

To practice beginning sounds, make up a sentence using as many words as possible that begin with the same consonant. Let the sentence be silly! Once you've made up one silly sentence, choose another consonant and make up another sentence. How silly can you get?

If you need help remembering the beginning consonants, use the list on page 6 to remind yourself.

A **simile** compares two things using the word *like* or *as.* For example, *as silly as a seal in sandals.* Make up your own similes, using words that begin with the same beginning consonants. Use the following simile starters, or make up your own!

as silly as . . .   as wet as . . .   as big as . . .

Remember This

A **mnemonic** (nee-MON-ik) is a rhyme or other trick that helps you remember something. You can use mnemonics to help you remember

Circle the **c** or **g** in each word. Then circle the letter that shows which sound the **c** or **g** spells.

1. came	s	k
2. page	g	j
3. voice	s	k
4. gave	g	j
5. place	s	k
6. gentle	g	j
7. carry	s	k
8. pig	g	j
9. icy	s	k
10. large	g	j

Answers on page 13.

POP QUIZ

how to spell difficult words. The rhyme "Use **i** before **e** except after **c** or when sounded as an **a** as in *neighbor* and *weigh*" is a mnemonic. You'll find many helpful mnemonics throughout this book. Look for a lightbulb, like the one below, to help you recognize them!

The best mnemonics are the ones you think up yourself. No matter how silly a mnemonic is, if it helps you, use it! Here's an example: *A rat in Tom's house might eat Tom's ice cream.* (Put together the first letter in each word to spell *arithmetic.* <u>A</u> <u>r</u>at <u>in</u> <u>Tom's</u> <u>h</u>ouse <u>m</u>ight <u>e</u>at <u>Tom's</u> <u>i</u>ce <u>c</u>ream.) Try writing your own mnemonic to help you remember a spelling pattern or the spelling of a particular word. Let a friend try your mnemonic. Does it help?

End at the Feet: Consonants at the End of Words

Many of the same consonant sounds and letters that begin words are also heard at the end of words, whether or not they are the last letter you see.

b—rub, cube	p—mop, rip
d—did, road	r—hear, car
f—if, fluff	s—bus, glass
k—bake	t—bat, hot
l—cool, fill	x—fix
m—bloom, gum	z—buzz
n—fun, fan	

What about consonants **c, g, h, j, q, w,** and **y?** This chart shows what happens when **c, g,** or **q** is found at the end of a word.

Consonant	Sound	Usual Spelling at the End of a Word	Examples
c	k	c, ck	traffic, brick
c	s	ce	advice
g	g	g	hug
g	j	ge	huge
q	k	que	plaque

The letters **h, w,** and **y** may appear at the end of words: *touch, rough, how, snow, saw, day, toy.* But they never spell the consonant sounds that they spell at the beginning of words.

juice
We like ju*ice ice* cold.

STRONG & SILENT

The letter **e** at the end of a one-syllable word often means that the word has a long vowel sound. (Listen to the difference in the vowel sounds in the words *hat* and *hate.*) You can read about long vowel sounds in Chapter 4.

Word Stairs

Write a word that begins and ends with consonant letters. Then think of a word that begins with the same consonant found at the end of the first word. Write the second word coming down from the last letter of the first word. Continue making "stairs" by writing a new word at the end of the last word. In this example, the word *top* uses the final **t** of *boot,* the word *pear* uses the final **p** in *top,* and so on.

BOOT
O
PEAR
A
TONE
V
E
R

What is found at the end of a rainbow?

Answer: The letter w.

Ha HA!

What About the Ribs? Consonants in the Middle of Words

We know that there are consonants at the beginning of words (the head) and at the end of words (the feet), but what about in the middle? Of course consonants appear in the middle of words too. We can't forget about the skeleton's ribs! (Think about the consonants **n, s,** and **n** in the middle of the word *consonant*.)

When you need to, you can divide words into sections called **syllables.** Each syllable can be said by itself. (*Itself* has two syllables: *it* and *self.*) Sometimes words have only one syllable, like *ant* or *tent*.

What happens once in a minute, twice in a moment, but never in a day?

Answer: The letter m.

The consonants that are in the middle of words are really at the beginning or end of syllables. (You'll learn more about syllables in Chapter 9.) Every syllable has a vowel sound, and most syllables, like many one-syllable words, begin or end with consonant sounds.

MIDDLE CHECKUP

Circle the two words in each set that have the same middle sound.

1. kitten   music   batter
2. zipper   pepper   cabin
3. camel   bacon   lemon
4. hotel   melon   pilot
5. medal   saddle   tiger

Answers on page 13.

POP QUIZ

mnemonic

consonant
There's an *ant* in conson*ant*.

mnemonic

balloon
Most balloons look like a *ball*.

Silent Letters

Sometimes a word has a consonant that does not spell a sound—it's silent. Silent letters can appear at the beginning, middle, or end of a word. Although silent letters don't make a sound, you still have to remember to include them in order to spell a word correctly.

Why is the letter t like a cold day?

Answer: Because it's in the middle of winter.

Ha HA!

POP QUIZ

SPELL CHECK

Correct the misspellings in each of these sentences.

1. My koat is at the jym.

_____

2. We have a qart of guice.

_____

3. Fil my glas.

_____

4. The wal is made of bric.

_____

Answers on page 13.

Silent Letter or Letters	Examples
b	thum**b**, clim**b**
d	ba**d**ge, he**d**ge
k	**k**now, **k**nock
g	si**g**n, **g**naw
h	r**h**yme, **g**host
l	cou**l**d, wou**l**d
t	whis**t**le, of**t**en
w	**w**rap, **w**ho
gh	bou**gh**t, thou**gh**

Practice Makes Perfect

To practice learning how to spell words with silent letters, try this. Write down a sentence that has at least one word with a silent letter. Then say the sentence out loud to a partner, who writes the sentence on a different sheet of paper. Check each other's work. If you don't get it right the first time, study the correct spelling for a moment and then try again.

By listening to the spoken word and then writing it down, you will picture the letters, helping you to learn the correct spelling.

page 6

Letter Riddle

If it takes five people one day to dig up a field, how long will it take ten people to dig up the same field?

Answer: No time at all! The field has already been dug up.

page 9

C and G Checkup

1) came (**k**), 2) page (**j**), 3) voice (**s**), 4) gave (**g**), 5) place (**s**), 6) gentle (**j**), 7) carry (**k**), 8) pig (**g**), 9) icy (**s**), 10) large (**j**)

page 11

Middle Checkup

1) kitten, batter; 2) zipper, pepper; 3) camel, lemon; 4) melon, pilot; 5) medal, saddle

page 12

Spell Check

1) My coat is at the gym. 2) We have a quart of juice. 3) Fill my glass. 4) The wall is made of brick.

Consonant Blends and Digraphs
Howdy, Partner!

Not all words begin or end with consonant sounds spelled by single consonants.
Sometimes consonants like to work together in pairs or groups!

It Takes Two: Consonant Blends

Suppose you are trying to write an exciting story. You have a sentence in your head that you want to write down:

The cows plodded slowly down the trail.

You can use what you know about spelling consonant sounds to help you spell *cows* and *down*. They begin with single consonants. But *plodded*, *slowly*, and *trail* begin with two consonants. Because the sounds spelled by the two consonants blend together, these pairs of consonants are called *blends*.

WHAT IS A BLENDED SOUND?

When two consonant sounds blend together, you can still hear both consonant sounds. But the two sounds together are a little different from each sound alone. Say the words *pay*, *lay*, and *play*. The blended sound at the beginning of *play* is made up of the **p** sound and the **l** sound, but as you can tell, the blended sound is different than both individual sounds.

On the next page are some consonant blends you will often see at the beginning of words. Many consonant blends are made up of a consonant followed by the letter **l** or **r**. These are called **l**-blends and **r**-blends. Other common consonant blends start with the letter **s** followed by another consonant. These are called **s**-blends.

Why did the teacher wear sunglasses in class? (Hint: Think br!)

Answer: Because her students were so bright.

Ha HA!

r-Blends	Examples	l-Blends	Examples	s-Blends	Examples
br	bread, brain	bl	blue, blend	sc	scale, scoop
cr	cry, crowd	cl	clap, climb	sk	sky, skate
dr	drop, drain	fl	fly, flower	sl	slide, slow
fr	fry, frown	gl	glad, globe	sm	small, smooth
gr	grin, grow	pl	plum, place	sn	snake, sneeze
pr	print, prove	sl	slow, sled	sp	space, spell
tr	try, true			st	store, sting
				sw	swing, swan

mnemonic

children
Exaggerate the pronunciation. Say *child/ren* so you won't forget the **ld**.

Go Fish for Blends

You'll need a bunch of blank 3×5 index cards to make word cards. Think of a word that starts with a consonant blend. Write this word on two different cards. Repeat this until you have 25 pairs of matching cards.

This game is just like Go Fish, but instead of looking for number pairs you are looking for beginning consonant blend pairs. Shuffle the cards, and give five cards to each player. Put the remaining cards in a facedown pile. The object of the game is to get the most matching pairs.

POP QUIZ

MAKE BLEND WORDS

Replace the blend at the beginning of the words with each of the blends shown to make new words.

Word Blends	New Words
1. clap	fl _____
	sl _____
2. trip	gr _____
	dr _____
3. snack	sm _____
	st _____
4. flock	cl _____
	bl _____
5. prim	br _____
	gr _____
6. sling	sw _____
	st _____

Answers on page 23.

What is full of holes but holds water? (Hint: Think sp!)
Answer: a sponge

First, each player lays down any matching pairs he or she has and picks replacement cards from the stack. The players then take turns asking each other for matches, for example, "Do you have *swing?*" If the player does have the matching card, they hand it over. If you do not get the card requested, pick one card from the pile. If you get a match, place the matched pair face down on the table and take another turn. If you don't get a match, it's the next player's turn. Whoever has the most pairs when all the cards are gone is the winner.

What is the hardest part about skydiving? (Hint: Think gr!)
Ha HA!
Answer: the ground

Two for One: Consonant Digraphs

Like a consonant blend, a consonant *digraph* is also a pair of consonants. But the two letters in a consonant digraph spell one sound, not two. This sound is usually different from the sound that either letter spells on its own. Listen to the beginning sound in *chair*. It's not the **k** sound or the **s** sound that **c** usually spells. And it's not the **h** sound that **h** usually spells.

Most consonant digraphs can spell more than one sound. The digraph **ch** can spell the sound in *chair* or the sound in *choir*. The digraph **th** can spell the sound in *that* or the sound in *thin*. (Listen closely to hear the difference.) The digraph **wh** can spell the sound in *whale* or the sound in *who*. Say each pair of words: *chair* and *choir*, *that* and *thin*, *whale* and *who*. Can you hear the difference in the beginning sounds?

Digraph	Examples
ch	**ch**air, **ch**oose *or* **ch**oir, **ch**ameleon
sh	**sh**ip, **sh**e
th	**th**em, **th**ose *or* **th**ank, **th**ing
wh	**wh**ale, **wh**y *or* **wh**o, **wh**ole

What ?
Who ?

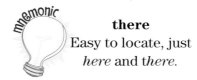

mn**e**monic

there
Easy to locate, just
here and *there.*

Author, Author!

Practice identifying and spelling digraphs with this activity. Pretend you're writing a story for your school newspaper. (Or write one for real! Wouldn't it be cool to have your work published?) Write about something that happened this week at school. When you are finished writing your draft, circle all the words with beginning consonant digraphs. How many are there? Which words did you use most often?

MAKE DIGRAPH WORDS

Finish each word by writing the digraph that spells the beginning sound in the picture name.

1. ____ake   ____eep   ____out

2. ____ump   ____aw   ____ick

3. ____art   ____eap   ____ild

4. ____eat   ____ere   ____ich

Answers on page 23.

POP QUIZ

GREEK IS THE WORD

Words that have the **k** sound spelled **ch** (*chorus, character*) and the **f** sound spelled **ph** (*phonics, photograph*) usually came into the English language from ancient Greek words.

What has four legs and a back but no body? (Hint: Think *ch*!)

HaHA!

Answer: a chair

What do garage mechanics wear to ballet class? (Hint: Think *sh*!)

Answer: tow shoes

Ha HA!

POP QUIZ

SPELLING BEE!

This is a little different from a regular spelling bee. Instead of listening to a word and then spelling it, use the beginning digraph and the clue to figure out what word to write.

1. ch   ham and _____ sandwich
2. sh   _____ and tell
3. wh   once in a _____
4. ch   _____ for the home team
5. th   first, second, _____
6. wh   black and _____ stripes

Answers on page 23.

When is hot soup not hot soup? (Hint: Think ch!)
Answer: When it's chili (chilly)!

Ha HA!

s-p-e-l-l-i-n-g

Two Plus One: Three-Letter Consonant Blends

Some consonant blends are made up of three sounds and three letters together. Look at the words *strike* and *spring*. How many consonants do you see at the beginning? What consonant sounds do those letters spell?

A few three-letter combinations are made up of a digraph and a consonant, so they spell only two sounds: *school, three.* And **squ** is a three-letter blend. Why? It doesn't have three consonants at the beginning, but it does have three letters that spell two sounds—**s** and **qu.**

Three-Letter Blends	Examples
chr	**Chr**istmas, **chr**ome
sch	**sch**edule, **sch**eme
scr	**scr**ub, **scr**eam
shr	**shr**ink, **shr**ed
spl	**spl**it, **spl**ash
spr	**spr**ay, **spr**out
squ	**squ**are, **squ**eak
str	**str**ing, **str**ipe
thr	**thr**ee, **thr**ead

mnemonic

school
*Ch*ildren go to s*ch*ool.

Know Your ABCs

Sorting words into alphabetical order (as long as they're spelled correctly) is a good way to practice spelling because it gives you a real reason to look at the individual letters. Write on separate slips of paper as many words as you can think of that begin with three-letter blends. (Check out the charts in this section or use a dictionary if you need help.) Then put the slips faceup on a desk or table and mix them up. As quickly as you can, put the words in alphabetical order. Do this two or three times, trying to do it faster each time. What was your fastest time?

It should come as no surprise that the more you practice this activity, the easier it will be for you to spell these words.

HaHA! *What did the horse say after finishing its hay?*
(Hint: Think of a word with a three-letter blend!)
Answer: "That's the last straw."

POP QUIZ

Be a Spelling Detective!

Hmm...one word is misspelled in each group of words. Can you find it? Circle the misspelled word and write it correctly.

1. thrill	chrome	shirimp	_____
2. squirm	splasch	street	_____
3. sprinkle	scratch	strech	_____
4. squeeze	skeme	spruce	_____
5. strong	skreen	sprawl	_____
6. thorough	threw	thret	_____
7. spred	strange	scroll	_____
8. strum	skwash	squirt	_____

Answers on page 23.

How did the eggs cross the road?
(Hint: Think of a word with a three-letter blend!)
Answer: They scrambled. **HaHA!**

End of the Trail: Final Consonant Combinations

Some of the consonant blends and digraphs that begin words are also found at the end of words.

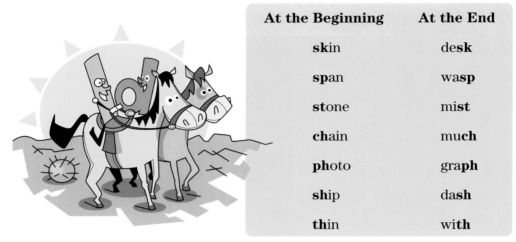

At the Beginning	At the End
s**k**in	des**k**
span	was**p**
s**t**one	mis**t**
chain	mu**ch**
photo	gra**ph**
ship	da**sh**
thin	wi**th**

But some pairs of consonants appear only at the end of words. They may be doubles (**ff, ll, ss**), digraphs (**nk, ng**), blends (**ct, ld, lf, lk, lt, mp, nd, nt, pt**), or none of these (**ck**). Blends and digraphs work the same way at the end of words as they do at the beginning: Blends spell blended sounds, and digraphs spell a different (new) sound. Double letters spell the same sound that they spell as a single letter. The letters **ss** spell the **s** sound, the letters **ll** spell the **l** sound, and so on. And the letters **ck** spell the **k** sound.

Final Consonant Combinations	Examples	Final Consonant Combinations	Examples
ch	bun**ch**, tea**ch**	ng	ra**ng**, lo**ng**
ck	ba**ck**, pi**ck**	nk	ba**nk**, shri**nk**
ct	fa**ct**, stri**ct**	nt	ce**nt**, pla**nt**
ff	pu**ff**, flu**ff**	ph	gra**ph**, sta**ph**
lf	she**lf**, wo**lf**	sh	bru**sh**, wa**sh**
lk	mi**lk**, e**lk**	sk	a**sk**, du**sk**
ll	ba**ll**, dri**ll**	sp	cri**sp**, wa**sp**
lt	be**lt**, sa**lt**	ss	bo**ss**, dre**ss**
mp	la**mp**, ju**mp**	st	be**st**, toa**st**
nd	a**nd**, ki**nd**	th	smoo**th**, tee**th**

SOUNDALIKE

The sounds of **ng** and **nk** are very much alike. Say *wing* and *wink*. Can you hear the difference in the ending sounds? When you say them, you can feel the difference in pronouncing the endings. Can you think of other pairs of words in which the only difference is that one word ends with **ng** and the other ends with **nk**? How about *bang* and *bank*, *rang* and *rank*, *sang* and *sank*, and *thing* and *think*? These are just a few examples. When spelling these words, pay close attention to the ending sounds so you don't substitute a wrong letter.

How do you make an egg roll?
(Hint: Think of a word with a final diagraph!)
Answer: Push it.

DIGRAPH CHALLENGE

Can you think of a word that begins and ends with the same consonant digraph? Write **ch__ch, sh__sh,** and **ph__ph** on a sheet of paper. Try thinking of a letter or letters that could go in the middle to make words.

Church, shush, and *photograph* each begin and end with the same consonant digraph.

PICK ONE

Fill in the blanks with the consonant combination that begins one word and ends the other word in each pair.

ch   sh   th   sk   sp   st

1. ___arp   bu___
2. ___erry   pea___
3. ___ill   bri___
4. ___and   wri___
5. ___ink   bo___
6. ___eck   gra___

Answers on page 23.

POP QUIZ

What do sharks eat with their peanut butter?
(Hint: Think of a word with a final digraph!)
Answer: Jellyfish

HaHA!

Consonants Working Together

Let's review what you have learned in this chapter:

 Consonant blends

—two or three consonants that spell a blended sound

—can be at the beginning or end of a word

 Consonant digraphs

—two consonants that spell a single, new sound

—can be at the beginning or end of a word

 Other consonant combinations

—double letters that appear at the end of a word

SPELL CHECK

Unscramble these words. Make sure each word begins *and* ends with a consonant blend, a consonant digraph, or a consonant combination. Remember to look for spelling patterns.

1. shbur
2. krtucs
3. dlebn
4. kchsa
5. sresd

6. alfhs
7. tciwsh
8. shtec
9. rnsigp
10. aktnh

Answers on page 23.

BE A SPELLING DETECTIVE!

Each group of words below contains one misspelled word. Find the misspelled word, and write it correctly. Watch out for consonant blends and digraphs!

1. brick	splash	fall	swinge	_____
2. scool	crisp	check	thing	_____
3. strict	shrimp	drensh	slash	_____
4. string	smart	skold	print	_____
5. whind	cling	boss	bunch	_____

Answers on page 23.

POP QUIZ ANSWERS

page 15

Make Blend Words
1) flap, slap; 2) grip, drip; 3) smack, stack; 4) clock, block; 5) brim, grim;
6) swing, sting

page 17

Make Digraph Words
1) shake, sheep, shout; 2) thump, thaw, thick; 3) chart, cheap, child; 4) wheat,
where, which

page 18

Spelling Bee!
1) cheese, 2) show, 3) while, 4) cheer, 5) third, 6) white

page 19

Be a Spelling Detective!
1) shrimp, 2) splash, 3) stretch, 4) scheme, 5) screen, 6) threat, 7) spread, 8) squash

page 21

Pick One
1) **sh** (*sharp* and *bush*), 2) **ch** (*cherry* and *peach*), 3) **sk** (*skill* and *brisk*), 4) **st** (*stand*
and *wrist*), 5) **th** (*think* and *both*), 6) **sp** (*speck* and *grasp*)

page 22

Spell Check
1) brush, 2) struck, 3) blend, 4) shack, 5) dress, 6) flash, 7) switch, 8) chest,
9) spring, 10) thank

page 22

Be a Spelling Detective!
1) swing, 2) school, 3) drench, 4) scold, 5) wind

Short Vowel Sounds
Meet the Team

Give me an a! Give me an e! Give me an i! Give me an o! Give me a u!
What have I got? The vowels!

The Five Vowels

Let's hear it for the five vowels! They are only 5 of the 26 letters in the alphabet, but they are very important in the English language. Without them, we wouldn't have any words at all.

What's that? Ah, you're thinking of Chapter 1! You thought we couldn't have words without consonants. Well, that's true, too. It takes consonants *and* vowels to make words. But think about this: Alone and together, the consonants spell about 65 different sounds. (You read about them in Chapters 1 and 2.) That seems like a lot of sounds, but remember, there are 21 consonants. And 38 of those sounds are blends of other sounds.

Alone and together, the five vowels spell about 15 different sounds. And at least one of those sounds occurs in every word in the English language.

OK, we've run through the stats. Now it's time to meet the team! Here are your vowels: **a, e, i, o,** and **u.** This chapter talks about the

WEE WORDS

Which vowels can also be words? Are there any consonants that can do that?

A and *I* are vowels that are also words. There are no consonants that spell words by themselves.

easiest vowel sounds to spell: the short vowel sounds. (They aren't really "short"—they take the same time to say as other vowel sounds.) Vowels are called short when they don't "say" their names or combine with the letter **r.** You'll see!

A SIXTH VOWEL?

The letter **y** is a sneaky spy. Usually it is a consonant. It stands for the sound you hear at the beginning of *yard* and *year.* But sometimes **y** acts like a vowel. Look at the first sentence in this paragraph. In *sneaky,* the **y** stands for the long **e** sound. In *spy,* it stands for the long **i** sound. When **y** sounds like **i,** it is a vowel, not a consonant. You'll meet **y** as a vowel in Chapter 4.

Up to Bat . . . It's Short a!

Say the word *cat* slowly. Listen carefully. How many sounds does *cat* have? That's right. It has three sounds. You hear one sound at the beginning. You hear one sound at the end. And you hear another sound in the middle—the short **a** vowel sound. Say *cat* again. Hold the middle sound, stretching it out. You want to be able to recognize that sound when you hear it. It is the short **a** sound, and it is spelled **a.**

CVC WORDS

Many words have the short **a** sound. The simplest short **a** words are like *cat.* They have three letters: The first letter is a consonant, the second letter is a vowel (**a**), and the third letter is a consonant. Consonant–vowel–consonant. That's why these words are called CVC words. And here's an important tip: Most CVC words have short vowel sounds. Why is that important?

It's important because that gives you a good idea of how to spell the vowel sound in the word, which helps you spell the word.

Look at this picture. Say its name. *Map.* How many sounds do you hear? What sound do you hear at the beginning? What sound do you hear at the end? Are these consonant sounds? Now you know this is a CVC word. The vowel sound in the middle is a short vowel sound. You listen to the sound, and you know that it is spelled **a**.

Tongue Twisters

Say these sentences quickly several times. You'll notice that most of the words contain the short **a** sound.

A mad lad had a hat.

A fat rat sat on a mat.

A bad cat grabbed a bat.

How many short **a**'s do you hear in these tongue twisters? There are 12 short **a** sounds: one each in the words *mad, lad, had, hat, fat, rat, sat, mat, bad, cat, grabbed,* and *bat.*

PICTURE NAMES

Write each picture name. Each one is a CVC word with a short **a** sound.

POP _____

_____

_____

WELCOME _____

TAXI _____

Answers on page 36.

(Hint: Think short **a**!)

Why are movie stars cool?

Answer: Because they have a lot of fans.

Ha HA!

Where do king crabs live?

Answer: in sand castles

HaHA!

POP QUIZ

You Bet! It's Short e!

Say the word *hen* slowly. Listen carefully to the middle sound. Say *hen* again. Hold the middle sound and stretch it out. That sound is the short **e** vowel sound. It is spelled **e**.

Now say the words *cat* and *hen*. Can you hear the difference in the vowel sounds? When you say *cat*, think: That is short **a**. It is spelled **a**. When you say *hen*, think: That is short **e**. It is spelled **e**. You want to be able to recognize these sounds whenever you hear them. You also want to remember the letters that spell the sounds.

Many CVC words have the short **e** vowel sound. You can use what you know about CVC words to help you spell them.

Look at this picture. Say its name. *Bed.* How many sounds do you hear? What sound do you hear at the beginning? What sound do you hear at the end? Are these consonant sounds? Now you know that this is a CVC word. The vowel sound in the middle is a short vowel sound. You listen to the sound, and you know that it is spelled **e**.

What did one pig say to the other pig? (Hint: Think short e!) Answer: "Let's be pen pals."

HaHA!

ANOTHER SPELLING FOR SHORT E

OK, so **e** spells the short **e** sound—most of the time.

Uh-oh! What does that mean?

Well, one thing about the English language is that while many words follow particular patterns (and learning these patterns can help you spell the words!), there are also a lot of words that *don't* follow a pattern—or they *do* follow a pattern, but it may not help you spell them. Usually you just have to memorize how to spell these words.

Why is a river lazy? (Hint: Think short e!) Answer: It doesn't get off its bed.

Ha HA!

Bread, head, health, thread. What vowel sound do you hear in these words? It's the short **e** sound. But what letters spell the short **e** sound in the words? Not just **e,** but the letters **ea** together.

ANOTHER SOUND FOR EA

Just to make things even more interesting, the letters **ea** can also spell the long **e** vowel sound (*each*) or the long **a** vowel sound (*great*). These letters can also be separate sounds (*Seattle*). And then there's *ocean.* . . . You'll find out more about **ea** in Chapter 4.

TRY IT OUT

Write each word next to the phrase that describes it.

heavy   wealthy   spread   ahead   breakfast   dead

1. not behind _____

2. cover an area _____

3. first meal _____

4. not alive _____

5. weighs a lot _____

6. not poor _____

Answers on page 36.

POP QUIZ

The words you wrote in "Try It Out" all have the short **e** sound spelled **ea.** Look at the words. Do you see anything that helps you know they have a different spelling for short **e?** Nope.

The easiest way to learn how to spell these words is simply to memorize them. Here are some more words in which **ea** spells the short **e** sound:

dread	feather	heaven	instead	leather
meant	ready	sweater	wealth	weather

What can you hold without using your hands?

(Hint: Think of a word in which ea spells the short e sound.)

Answer: your breath

Ha HA!

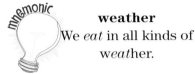

mnemonic

weather
We *eat* in all kinds of w*ea*ther.

Winning Tips for Short i!

Say the word *pig* slowly. How many sounds do you hear? What sound do you hear at the beginning? Is that a consonant sound? What sound do you hear at the end? Is that a consonant sound? So what kind of sound do you expect to hear in the middle? That's right—a short vowel sound. (Because the word *pig* has three sounds, and the beginning and ending sounds are consonant sounds, *pig* must be a CVC word. And since most CVC words have short vowel sounds, *pig* will probably have a short vowel sound.)

Now… which short vowel sound does *pig* have? Is it the short **a** sound in *cat?* Say *cat* and *pig.* No, it's not short **a.** Is it the short **e** sound in *hen?* Say *hen* and *pig.* No, it's not short **e.**

The sound in the middle of *pig* is the short **i** vowel sound.

THINGS TO DO

Complete each sentence with a CVC word that has the short **i** sound.

1. We are going to _____ a hole in the yard.

2. I want to _____ the hole with dirt.

3. Jordan _____ the ball with the bat.

4. Aunt Sybil needs to _____ down on the chair.

5. The best team will _____ the game next week.

Answers on page 36.

POP QUIZ

Have you heard the joke about the jump rope? (Hint: Think short i!)

Answer: Skip it.

Ha HA!

HELP! IS IT I OR E?

Some people have trouble hearing the difference between short **e** and short **i**. Some people pronounce the two sounds the same. Say these pairs of words: *pin* and *pen, tin* and *ten, sit* and *set, pit* and *pet*. Say each word slowly. Stretch out the vowel sound. Compare that sound to the vowel sound in *pig* or *hen*. Say *pin* and *pig, pen* and *hen*. Then say *pin* and *pen* again. Can you hear the difference? Are you saying two different sounds?

If you still don't hear a difference, think about the meaning. The context, or meaning needed, will always make it plain whether the spelling is **i** or **e**.

Why did the pelican refuse to pay for his meal? (Hint: Think short i!)

Answer: His bill was too big.

HaHA!

Follow the a, e, i Vowels

Follow the path of short vowel words. Begin at START. Read aloud the first word. Name the vowel sound in the word. Think of another word that has the same vowel sound, and write that word in the blank. Move on to the next box.

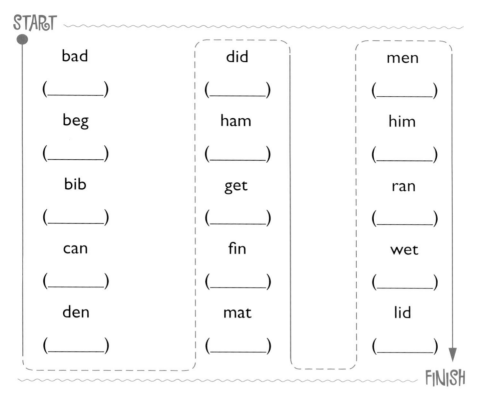

START

bad

(_____)

beg

(_____)

bib

(_____)

can

(_____)

den

(_____)

did

(_____)

ham

(_____)

get

(_____)

fin

(_____)

mat

(_____)

men

(_____)

him

(_____)

ran

(_____)

wet

(_____)

lid

(_____)

FINISH

Oh, My Gosh! It's Short o!

Say the word *fox* slowly. How many sounds do you hear? Is the first sound a consonant sound? Is the last sound a consonant sound? So you expect that the middle sound will be . . . Right! A short vowel sound!

We've discussed three short vowel sounds already: short **a**, short **e**, and short **i**. Does *fox* have any of these vowel sounds? Let's find out. Say *fox* and *cat*. Listen to the vowel sounds. Are they the same?

No. Say *fox* and *hen.* Are the vowel sounds the same? No. Say *fox* and *pig.* Are the vowel sounds the same? No again. The vowel sound in *fox* is different. It is the short **o** vowel sound.

POP QUIZ

RHYMING WORDS

Write two words that rhyme with each word. Notice how you spell the vowel sound in each word.

1. hot _____ _____

2. pop _____ _____

3. nod _____ _____

4. cob _____ _____

5. dog _____ _____

Answers on page 37.

BUILD WORDS

Add **a, e, i,** or **o** to each word pattern. How many words can you make?

b __ t   s __ t   t __ p

b __ g   h __ t   p __ t

Short a	**Short e**	**Short i**	**Short o**

Answers on page 37.

POP QUIZ

Give It Up for Short u!

By now you know how this works. Say the word *bug* slowly. Does it have three sounds? Does it have consonant sounds at the beginning and the end? Do you think its vowel sound will be short? Yes, yes, and yes! *Bug* is a CVC word. It has a short vowel sound. But what short vowel sound?

Say *cat*, *hen*, *pig*, and *fox*. Then say *bug*. Does the vowel sound in *bug* sound like any of the other vowel sounds? No. The vowel sound in *bug* is the short **u** sound. It is spelled by the letter **u.**

Remember, the easier it is for you to recognize the short vowel sounds, the easier it will be for you to spell words containing these sounds.

FUN WITH SHORT U

Choose the short **u** word that finishes the answer to each riddle.

rough   mud   stumped   stuck   lunch

1. What did the dirt say to the rain?
   "If this keeps up, my name will be _____."

2. What did the tree say when it was cut down?
   "Well, I'm _____."

3. What did one plate say to the other plate?
   "_____ is on me."

4. What did the fly say to the flypaper?
   "I'm _____ on you."

5. What did the dog say when it sat on the sandpaper?
   "_____! _____!"

Answers on page 37.

POP QUIZ

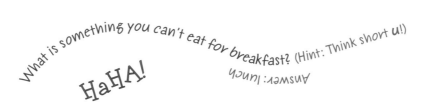

What is something you can't eat for breakfast? (Hint: Think short **u**!)

HaHA!

Answer: lunch

OTHER SPELLINGS FOR SHORT U

The short **u** sound also can be spelled by the letter **o**: *son, ton, come, some, done.* And the short **u** sound can be spelled by the letters **ou** together: *rough, tough, enough.* Your best bet for learning how to spell these words is—you guessed it—to memorize them.

There's More to CVC Words than C

Do you remember learning about consonant blends and digraphs in Chapter 2? Well, words that begin and end with consonant blends and digraphs often have short vowel sounds. That's because the two consonants in the blend or digraph act like one consonant. So the words are just like CVC words—even though they are really CCVC, CVCC, or even CCVCC words. Whew! Check out the examples below.

Short Vowel Sound	Words
a	trap, path, black
e	step, deck, spend
i	slip, wish, bring
o	chop, dock, blond
u	plum, dust, crumb

What does a boxer drink? (Hint: Think short **u**!)

Answer: punch

HaHA!

What's the best day to go to the beach? (Hint: Think short **u**!)

Answer: Sunday

Ha HA!

The Short Vowel Team

Let's hear it for the vowels! You've met the whole team, and you've found out that the five vowels can spell five short vowel sounds. Now it's time to work out with all five of those letters and sounds.

STORY TIME

Read the paragraph below. Circle all the words that have short vowel sounds. Write the words in the chart below according to their vowel sound. (Write each word only once.)

A man and his dog went for a walk. They walked around the block. The dog sniffed at the grass and the trees. The man looked up at the sun. It felt good on his face. He sat down on a bench. The dog flopped down next to him. They watched the kids run in the park. It looked like fun.

Short a	Short e	Short i	Short o	Short u

Answers on page 37.

SPELL CHECK

There are 13 misspelled words in the paragraph below, and they all have short vowel sounds. So listen for short vowel sounds as you read! Cross out each misspelled word and write the word correctly. Then circle all the words with short vowel sounds.

My pet is not like the pits most kids have. It is not a dug or a cat. It is a duck. Its name is Quack. I brag about Quack. He does trecks. My mom and dod get a kack out of Quack. Quack jimps up on the dosk and quicks for crombs. Quack can be lots of fun. Last week he hid nixt to a big plont. He quacked and ran whin I saw hom!

Answers on page 37.

POP QUIZ

POP QUIZ ANSWERS

page 26
Picture Names
can, hat, fan, mat, cab

page 28
Try It Out
1) ahead, 2) spread, 3) breakfast, 4) dead, 5) heavy, 6) wealthy

page 30
Things to Do
1) dig, 2) fill, 3) hit, 4) sit, 5) win

page 32

Rhyming Words
Possible answers: 1) cot, dot; 2) hop, mop; 3) rod, pod; 4) job, rob; 5) hog, log

page 32

Build Words

Short a	Short e	Short i	Short o
bat	bet	bit	hot
bag	beg	big	top
sat	set	sit	pot
hat	pet	hit	
tap		tip	
pat		pit	

page 33

Fun with Short u
1) mud, 2) stumped, 3) lunch, 4) stuck, 5) rough

page 35

Story Time

Short a	Short e	Short i	Short o	Short u
man	went	his	dog	up
and	felt	sniffed	block	sun
at	bench	it	on	run
grass	next	him	flopped	fun
sat		kids		
		in		

page 36

Spell Check
My pet is not like the pets most kids have. It is not a dog or a cat. It is a duck. Its name is Quack. I brag about Quack. He does tricks. My mom and dad get a kick out of Quack. Quack jumps up on the desk and quacks for crumbs. Quack can be lots of fun. Last week he hid next to a big plant. He quacked and ran when I saw him!

Long Vowel Sounds
The Team Returns

Here come the five vowels again. . . . But wait! They sound different than they did in Chapter 3. There the sounds they made were short. Here they are long.

Long Vowel Sounds

You already know that the five vowel letters can spell the five short vowel sounds. These letters can also spell the five long vowel sounds. What are the long vowel sounds? Just say the names of the five vowel letters: **a, e, i, o, u.** There—you've said the five long vowel sounds. The long vowel sounds are the same as the names of the vowel letters.

Now look at these pictures. Say each picture name, and listen carefully to the vowel sound in each word.

These words have the five long vowel sounds. Say the words several times. Make sure you can hear the differences in the vowel sounds. Each time you say a word, say to yourself: "This is long **a** (or **e** or **i** or **o** or **u**)." Recognizing the vowel sound in each word will make it easier to spell.

Long Vowel Spelling Patterns

In Chapter 3 you learned that most words with a CVC (consonant–vowel–consonant) pattern have short vowel sounds. Well, now you will learn some letter patterns that will help you tell about words with long vowel sounds.

CVCE WORDS

Cake is an example of a CVCe word. It has a consonant, a vowel, a consonant, and an **e** at the end. Say *cake*. How many sounds do you hear? That's right. It has three sounds. Hey, wait a minute... *cake* has four letters! It does have four letters, but the **e** at the end is silent; it does not spell a sound. Just because the **e** is silent doesn't mean it's not important, though. The silent **e** tells you that the **a** spells the long **a** vowel sound in *cake*.

The silent **e** is so powerful that it can change an entire word. Just watch.... **m–a–n** spells *man;* add a silent **e,** and you've got *mane!*

SHORT TO LONG

Adding an **e** to the end of some CVC words (with short vowel sounds) makes them into CVCe words with long vowel sounds. Look at the example below, then write the other words to finish the pairs.

CVC Words	CVCe Words
can	cane
tap	_____
_____	hate
bit	_____
_____	kite
hop	_____
_____	cube

Answers on page 51.

POP QUIZ

Read the CVC words from the Short to Long quiz (*left*) out loud. What vowel sounds do they have? Now read the CVCe words out loud. What vowel sounds do they have?

Adding an **e** at the end of *tap, bit,* and *hop* turns them into *tape, bite,* and *hope.* But taking the **e** away from *hate, kite,* and *cube* makes them *hat, kit,* and *cub.*

HERE COMES THE "BUT..."

Of course, there are exceptions to the CVCe pattern! Look at the words *have* and *give.* They are CVCe words, but they have short vowel sounds. You will need to add these words to your "Need to Memorize" list.

CVVC OR CVV WORDS

Leaf is an example of a CVVC word. It has two vowel letters in the middle. Say *leaf.* How many sounds do you hear? Only three sounds, right? That's because the two vowel letters, **ea,** together spell the vowel sound in *leaf.* When two vowels together spell one sound, they are called a **vowel digraph.** Vowel digraphs often spell long vowel sounds. The vowel digraph **ea** spells the long **e** sound in *leaf.*

CV WORDS

In CV words, the vowel usually spells a long vowel sound. And don't forget—consonant blends and digraphs are formed by two consonant letters, but they spell one consonant sound. Also remember that sometimes the letter **y** can act like a vowel. In the sentence "*So we fly,*" every word is a CV word!

Long e	Long i	Long o
be	by	go
he	my	no
me	fly	so
we	shy	
she	why	

So we fly.

Ways to Spell Long a

As you might expect, there is more than one way to spell the long **a** sound. The long **a** sound can be spelled with other vowels—but it takes a combination of two other vowels to make one long **a!**

- **CVCe.** This pattern is a very common way to spell words with the long **a** vowel sound. Think *cake, face, shape.* These words all use the **a–e** pattern. Can you think of any other CVCe words with the long **a** sound? There are dozens! (Remember, C can be either a consonant, a consonant blend, or a digraph.)

- **CVVC and CVV.** The vowel digraphs that most often spell the long **a** vowel sound are **ai** and **ay.** (Remember, sometimes the letter **y** acts like a vowel. It often works with another vowel to spell a vowel sound.)

Less common vowel digraphs that spell the long **a** sound are **ei** and **ea** and **ey**. (You've met **ea** before. Think back to Chapter 3, when you learned that **ea** also spells the short **e** vowel sound.)

ai	ay	ei	ea	ey
train	day	eight	break	hey
mail	stay	vein	great	obey
chain	clay	rein	steak	
fail	gray	sleigh		
paid	may			
paint	play			
rain	say			
sail	today			
wait	way			

So Which Goes with Which?

OK, so now we know that **a–e, ai, ay, ei,** and **ea** all can spell the long **a** sound. But which pattern spells the long **a** sound in a particular word? There is no hard and fast rule. There's nothing that tells you how to spell the long **a** in *cake*. Actually, *caik, cayk, ceak, ceik,* and *ceyk* all could be possible spellings. They're wrong, of course, but how's a person to know it?

Answers on page 51.

LONG A PATTERN CHECK

These words all have the long **a** vowel sound. What letters spell the vowel sound in each word? Circle the letters.

grace	snail	sway
spray	quake	braid
freight	gray	raise
blade	weigh	scrape

POP QUIZ

mnemonic

grateful
We are *grateful* to *Kate*.

There are a few hints that can help you narrow down the choices. The **a–e** and **ai** digraphs are the most common spellings for long **a**, so they are the ones you should try first. And **ay** generally appears only at the end of words or syllables. And a **c** followed by an **e** usually spells the **s** sound, not the **k** sound. After that, it's time to check the dictionary!

POP QUIZ

RIDDLE ME THIS

Figure out the answer to each riddle by writing **a–e, ai,** or **ay** in the blanks.

1. What bird can lift the most? A cr___n___.

2. What belongs to you but is used more by others?
   Your n___m___.

3. What is nothing but holes tied to holes yet is strong as iron?
   A ch___n.

4. What goes up but never comes down? Your ___g___.

5. What is the difference between the rising and the setting sun?
   A d___.

Answers on page 51.

What do people do in a clock factory?

(Hint: Think long a!)

Answer: They make faces all day.

HaHA!

Leaf!

Ways to Spell Long e

As with long **a**, there is also more than one way to spell long **e**.

• **CVCe.** There aren't many CVCe words that have the long e vowel sound. You might think of the name *Pete*. And some longer words, such as *complete*, *athlete*, and *delete*, contain the CVCe pattern with the long e sound. But the thing to remember is that CVCe is just not a common pattern for long e words.

• **CV.** Some very common long **e** words have this pattern. You met them earlier in the chapter, remember? These words include *be, we, he, she,* and *me.* Luckily, because these words are short and sweet (just two or three letters!), they are pretty easy to spell.

• **CVVC and CVV.** The most common spellings for the long **e** vowel sound are the vowel digraphs **ee** and **ea.**

ee	ea
green	beach
sleep	eat
keep	read
seem	clean
street	each
see	cheap

There's no easy way to know when to use **ee** and when to use **ea.** In fact, there are lots of **ee** and **ea** homophones. (Homophones are words that sound alike but have different spellings and meanings. You'll learn more about them in Chapter 8.) Think about *week* and *weak, heel* and *heal,* and *peek* and *peak.* You'll need to know which word you mean to use and how to spell it. It doesn't do you any good to spell the wrong version of the word on a spelling test!

Other vowel digraphs that can spell the long **e** sound are **ie** and **ei.** You're probably wondering how you'll know which one to use. Do you remember the following mnemonic from Chapter 1?

Use **i** before **e**
except after **c**
or when sounded as an **a**
as in *neighbor* or *weigh.*

VERY BUSY EA

The vowel digraph **ea** really gets around! It can spell three different vowel sounds: short **e** *(head)*, long **a** *(break)*, and long **e** *(bead)*. But most often it spells the long **e** sound.

In other words, use **ie** most of the time to spell the long **e** sound, but use **ei** if the long **e** sound comes after the letter **c.** (And as you read earlier, use **ei** to spell the long **a** sound, as in *reindeer* and *sleigh.*)

Of course, there are exceptions to this rule. No surprise there! You will have to memorize the spellings of words that don't follow these rules, such as *either* and *friend.*

ie	ei
brief	ceiling
field	receive
niece	seize
chief	
piece	

SILLY LONG E POEM

Read the poem out loud. Underline the words that have the long **e** sound, and circle the letters that spell the long **e** sound.

Do bees ever sneeze?

Do fleas have knees?

I wish someone could tell me, please.

Do bees like cheese?

Do fleas eat peas?

Who can answer questions like these?

Answers on page 51.

believe
Do you
bel*ieve* St*e*ve?

piece
A *piece* of *pie*

HaHA! A butcher is six feet tall. What does he weigh? (Hint: Think long *e*!)
Answer: meat

What kind of shoes do spies wear? (Hint: Think long *e*!)
Answer: sneakers

Ha HA!

Ways to Spell Long i

You're not thinking there's only one way to spell long **i**, are you? Looking at the different ways to spell long **a** and long **e** should give you a pretty good idea that there's more to **i** than just **i**.

• **CVCe.** Like long **a**, long **i** is also found in lots of CVCe words. Think *bike*, *fire*, *shine*, and *white*, for just a few examples. How many more can you think of?

• **CV.** Many common words are made up of a consonant, consonant digraph, or consonant blend and the letter **y**. You met some of them earlier in this chapter, as a matter of fact. Remember, in these words, the **y** acts like a vowel. It spells the long **i** sound. Words in this group include *by, shy, cry, sky,* and *why,* to name a few.

Because they have the same ending sound, the words above rhyme. As practice to help you remember which words have a **y** to spell the long **i** sound, create some simple rhyming poems using long **i** CV words. Here's an example:

See the kite fly
High in the sky.

Now it's your turn! Choose two long **i** words, and write a poem.

Long i spelled ie
die
lie
pie
tie

• **CVV.** The vowel digraph **ie** also can spell the long **i** sound. Hey... wait just a minute! If you're thinking that you just learned that **ie** spells the long **e** sound (page 43), you're right. Most of the time **ie** *does* spell the long **e** sound, but in a few words, **ie** spells long **i**.

• **Other Long i Patterns: igh, i(ld) and i(nd).** Say this word: *night.* How many sounds do you hear? How many letters do you see? *Night* has three sounds, but five letters. So, not every letter spells a sound. In words such as *night,* the letters **igh** combine to spell the long **i** sound.

igh	i(ld)	i(nd)
bright	child	blind
fight	mild	find
light	wild	grind
might		kind
right		mind
sigh		

Say these words: *child, find.* They have three sounds; they have the CVC pattern... but they don't have short vowel sounds. Why not? In these words, the consonant blends **ld** and **nd** signal that the **i** spells the long **i** vowel sound.

If two's company and three's a crowd, what's four and five? (Hint: Think long **i**!) Answer: nine

Ha HA!

WHAT'S WITH GH?

When **g** and **h** are on their own, they spell consonant sounds, just like all the other consonants. But when they get together, they have an identity problem! Sometimes they spell the **f** sound, as in *cough* and *rough*. Sometimes they combine with **i** to spell the long **i** sound, as in *night*.

Sometimes they don't have any sound, but they give a clue to the word's vowel sound, as in *weight*. And in at least two words, they spell the hard **g** sound. Can you name these words? Here are some hints:

haunts houses   *tastes good with tomato sauce*

A *ghost* haunts houses, and *spaghetti* is delicious with tomato sauce.

OR IT COULD BE VAN "GOG"!

Have you heard of the famous painter Vincent van Gogh? He was Dutch. Americans say his last name "Van Go." The British say it "Van Goff." The Dutch say it more like "Fun Khokh"! The Dutch pronunciation is probably closest to the way **gh** was pronounced in English hundreds of years ago.

RIDDLE ME THIS

Figure out the rhyming answers to each riddle. Of course, the answers contain words with the long **i** sound. (Make sure you spell the answers correctly!)

1. What is green and worth ten cents?

   a _____ _____

2. What might you call a kid who misbehaves?

   a _____ _____

3. What do you have when you are a little bit scared?

   a _____ _____

4. What is another name for the moon?

   a _____ _____

Answers on page 51.

POP QUIZ

Ways to Spell Long o

And how many ways are there to spell long **o**?

- **CVCe.** By now, you recognize the CVCe pattern, right? So you can probably guess that the letters **o** and **e** in many CVCe words spell the long **o** sound. And they do—nearly all the time. Watch out for words in which the letter v comes before the final **e**. Sometimes these words have the long **o** sound, as in *drove*, *grove*, and *stove*. But sometimes these words have the short **u** sound, as in *glove*, *love*, and *shove*.

- **CV.** Several very common CV words have the long **o** sound. Can you think of any? How about *go*, *no*, and *so?*

- **CVVC.** One vowel digraph that spells the long **o** sound is **oa**. Another is **ow**. The consonant **w** sometimes acts like a vowel when it is paired with a vowel letter. The vowel digraph **oe** also spells the long **o** sound in a few words.

Look at the table to the right. What do you notice about where the digraphs **oa** and **ow** appear in long **o** words? The **oa** appears in the middle of the words, and the **ow** and **oe** usually appear at the end of the words.

oa	ow	oe
boat	blow	doe
coach	bowl	foe
goal	crow	hoe
float	flow	toe
groan	grow	
load	know	
oak	low	
road	row	
soak	show	
throat	snow	
toast	slow	
soap	throw	

WHICH DIGRAPH?

Write the digraph **oa, ow,** or **oe** to finish each long **o** word.

f____m

r____st

thr____n

l____f

h____

bl____

Answers on page 51.

POP QUIZ

• **Other Long o Patterns: o(ld), o(ll), o(lt), and o(st).** The consonant blends **ld, ll, lt,** and **st** after an **o** often signal that the **o** spells the long **o** sound. But not always! Watch out for *cost*, *lost*, and *frost*.

Poets Know It

A great way to practice long **o** spellings is to become a poet. Really! It's not as hard as it sounds. Just make up a few simple rhyming sentences with long **o** words. Here are a few verses to get you started. Complete each rhyme with a long **o** word that rhymes with the underlined word. When you're done with these, make up a few more of your own.

o(ld)	o(ll)	o(lt)	o(st)
bold	poll	bolt	ghost
cold	roll	colt	host
fold	toll	jolt	most
gold	stroll	volt	post
hold			
mold			
old			
sold			
told			

To get down this <u>slope</u>,
I'll need a long _____.

Be careful, <u>Toad</u>,
When you cross the _____.

Fast flies a <u>crow</u>,
But a snail is _____.

In the story he <u>told</u>,
He looked for _____.

What can you put into a barrel full of water to make it lighter? (Hint: Think long o!) Answer: a hole

Ha HA!

What falls in winter but never gets hurt? (Hint: Think long o) Answer: snow

HaHA!

Ways to Spell Long u

Poor long **u**! There just aren't as many words with the long **u** sound as there are with the other long vowel sounds. But there's more than one way to spell long **u** in these words, of course!

• **CVCe.** Only a few long **u** words are CVCe words; for example, *cube*, *cute*, *huge*, *mule*, and *use*.

Cube!

• **CVV.** The digraph **ue** can spell the long **u** sound in *cue*. And the digraph **ew** spells the long **u** sound in *few* and *new*. But usually these digraphs spell the vowel sound you hear in *room*.

• **Other Long u Patterns:** Often the letter **u** spells the long **u** sound. But that happens only in words that have more than one syllable, for example, *unit*, *bugle*, *music*, and *menu*.

What can't you see that is always before you? (Hint: Think long u!) Answer: your future

Ha HA!

So Long to the Long Vowels!

You already knew that the five vowels can spell the five short vowel sounds (Chapter 3). And now you know that the same five vowels, when they are put together in different patterns, can spell the five long vowel sounds. Let's review the main spelling patterns for the long vowel sounds.

Long a	Long e	Long i	Long o	Long u
a–e	ee	i–e	o–e	u–e
ai	ea	y	oa	u
ay	ie	ie	ow	
ei	ei	igh	o(ld), (ll), (lt), (st)	

PATTERN CHECK

What letter or letters spell the long vowel sound in each word? Circle the letters.

sweep	flies	receive	shake
scroll	fuel	try	be
fuse	throat	play	value
grown	field	mold	bright
grain	scold	gleam	cube
slide	pupil	wild	close

Answers on page 51.

POP QUIZ

Why did the shy conductor stand with his back to the orchestra? (Hint: Think long **u**!)

HaHA!

Answer: He couldn't face the music.

The more often you see a word, the more likely you will be to remember how to spell it. With that in mind, it makes sense that reading is a good way to learn spelling. So in order to become a better speller, try reading as many things as you can get your hands on! Here's a fun activity to get you started and to help you practice the long vowel words—but make sure you check with your parents before you begin. They may not want you to take a scissors to their newspaper—especially if they're not finished with it yet!

Look through a newspaper. Read the headlines, and cut out all the words that have long vowel sounds. Sort the words into groups according to their long vowel sounds. Then sort each long vowel group into smaller groups according to the spellings of the long vowel sound.

Long Vowel Match

To make a set of long vowel cards, write the words *came, date, chain, mail, hay, ray, sleep, feet, each, clean, thief, field, hide, ripe, cry, shy, find, blind, sigh, tight, hold, gold, globe, hole, goat, soak, glow, tow, huge,* and *mute* on index cards, one word on a card. Shuffle the cards and place them facedown in a stack. Take the top card and read the word. Then take the next card. If the words have the same long vowel sound, keep the card and take two more cards. If they don't have the same long vowel sound, place them in a discard pile. Play passes to the next player. When all the cards have been matched, mix the cards and play again. This time, match cards that have the same long vowel sound *and* spelling pattern.

POP QUIZ ANSWERS

page 39

Short to Long
tap ➡ tape, hat ➡ hate, bit ➡ bite, kit ➡ kite, hop ➡ hope, cub ➡ cube

page 41

Long a Pattern Check
grace, snail, sway, spray, quake, braid, freight, gray, raise, blade, weigh, scrape

page 42

Riddle Me This
1) crane, 2) name, 3) chain, 4) age, 5) day

page 44

Silly Long e Poem
Do <u>bees</u> ever <u>sneeze</u>?
Do <u>fleas</u> have <u>knees</u>?
I wish someone could tell <u>me, please</u>.
Do <u>bees</u> like <u>cheese</u>?
Do <u>fleas</u> eat <u>peas</u>?
Who can answer questions like <u>these</u>?

page 46

Riddle Me This
1) a lime dime, 2) a wild child, 3) a slight fright, 4) a night light

page 47

Which Digraph?
foam, roast, thrown, loaf, hoe, blow

page 49

Pattern Check
sweep, flies, receive, shake, scroll, fuel, try, be, fuse, throat, play, value, grown, field, mold, bright, grain, scold, gleam, cube, slide, pupil, wild, close

Rhyming Words and Word Families
Rhyme Time

**Hickory, dickory, dock
The mouse ran up the clock.**

This is part of a Mother Goose rhyme. Did you know
that rhyming can help you spell words?

When Do Words Rhyme?

Words that rhyme have the same ending sounds. That doesn't
mean just the very last sound—it means the last vowel sound as
well as the last consonant sound or sounds. Say *cat* and *hat*.
They rhyme because they have the same vowel sound and the
same final consonant sound. Now say *hat* and *hit*. They have
the same final consonant sound, but they don't rhyme. That's
because they don't have the same vowel sound. Now say *hit*
and *hip*. They don't rhyme either. They have the same vowel
sound but not the same final consonant sound.

Rhyming words can be useful to spellers. How? Say you know how
to spell *cat*. You know that **c** spells the **k** sound, **a** spells the
short **a** sound, and **t** spells the **t** sound. Then you hear a new
word that rhymes with *cat*. Right away you figure that the
word's vowel sound is spelled **a** and its final consonant
sound is spelled **t,** because that's how the sounds are
spelled in *cat*. Now all you have to do is figure out which letter
spells the word's beginning sound.

Of course, there are exceptions. Some sounds can have different spellings. Say
the words *tree* and *tea*. They rhyme, but that won't help you with their spellings.
That's because the long **e** sound can be spelled in more than one way. Even so,
there are many, many words that rhyme *and* have the same spellings for the last
vowel sound and the last consonant sound or sounds. So many, in fact, that they
can be grouped into word families according to their *phonograms*. Phonogram
is a fancy way of saying "the spelling for the last vowel sound and the last
consonant sound or sounds." For example, the phonogram in *cat* and *hat* is **-at.**

Short a Word Families

Let's build a word family. We already have two **-at** words, *cat* and *hat*. So let's make a list of words with the **-at** phonogram. The easiest way to think of rhyming words is to take a word (such as *cat*), change the consonant or consonants at the beginning of the word, and see if that makes a real word. First, go through the consonants in alphabetical order. Next, try making words using consonant blends and digraphs. Write down all the real words.

Consonant -at	Blend or digraph -at
bat	brat
cat	chat
fat	flat
hat	scat
mat	slat
pat	spat
rat	that
sat	
vat	

That's 16 words you can spell because you know how to spell the **-at** phonogram and beginning consonant sounds.

Use the same steps to build word families for **-an** and **-ap.** (You don't need to come up with every single **-an** and **-ap** word; this is just for practice.)

Words with -an	Words with -ap
_____an	_____ap
_____an	_____ap
_____an	_____ap
_____an	_____ap
_____an	_____ap
_____an	_____ap

Did you think of any of these words? *can, fan, man, ran, van, plan, than;* and *cap, map, nap, tap, clap, slap, snap, trap.* You probably thought of some that aren't included in those lists, as well. Of course, there are many other words in these word families.

Have fun practicing spelling words in the **-at, -an,** and **-ap** word families by making up a few silly rhymes. Here's an example:

No matter where he ran,
He couldn't find the van.

WORD FAMILY SORT

Sort these words into word families by writing each word in the correct column.

gap	slam	wrap	swam	trap
clash	stamp	flash	cramp	camp
lamp	sap	ramp	mash	trash
jam	cash	clam	chap	ram

-am	**-ap**	**-amp**	**-ash**

Answers on page 62.

POP QUIZ

(Hint: Answer these riddles by thinking of short **a** words that rhyme.)

What do you call an angry boy?

Answer: a mad lad

Ha HA!

What do you call potato chips for ducks?

Answer: a quack snack

HaHA!

THE GOOD OLD DAYS

Up until the end of the fifteenth century, people spelled English words pretty much any way they wished. They even made up their own spellings!

Short e Word Families

You know what word families are, and you know how to make them. So build word families for these short **e** phonograms. Remember, try different consonants, consonant digraphs, and blends at the beginning.

Words with -ed	Words with -en	Words with -ell	Words with -et
____ed	____en	____ell	____et
____ed	____en	____ell	____et
____ed	____en	____ell	____et
____ed	____en	____ell	____et
____ed	____en	____ell	____et
____ed	____en	____ell	____et

Possible words include *bed, fed, led, sled, sped; hen, men, pen, ten, then; bell, fell, sell, tell, yell, shell, spell;* and *bet, get, jet, pet, wet.* If you thought of any other words, good for you!

USE THE CLUES

Write the short **e** word that goes with each clue. Then circle the phonogram in the word.

1. something you sleep on _____
2. the number after nine _____
3. what you use your nose for _____
4. the plural form of *man* _____
5. the opposite of *dry* _____
6. to shout loudly _____

Answers on page 62.

POP QUIZ

Change a Letter, Change a Word

Write one of these words at the top of a column: *can, bag, red,* or *pen.* Make the word into another word by changing only one letter. Write the second word under the first one. Then make the second word into another word by changing only one letter again. Continue in this way. See how long a chain of words you can make! Here's part of a chain:

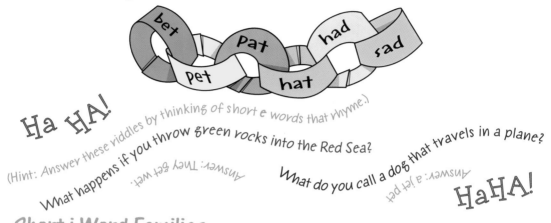

Ha HA!

(Hint: Answer these riddles by thinking of short e words that rhyme.)

What happens if you throw green rocks into the Red Sea?

Answer: They get wet.

What do you call a dog that travels in a plane?

Answer: a jet pet

HaHA!

Short i Word Families

Gosh, look at how many words you have already made! And you've only used **a** and **e!** Keep going. Build word families for these short **i** phonograms.

Words with -ig	Words with -it	Words with -in	Words with -ip
____ig	____it	____in	____ip
____ig	____it	____in	____ip
____ig	____it	____in	____ip
____ig	____it	____in	____ip
____ig	____it	____in	____ip
____ig	____it	____in	____ip

How many words did you come up with? Possible answers include *big, dig, fig, pig; fit, hit, kit, quit, sit, spit; fin, pin, tin, win, chin, grin; dip, hip, tip, zip, chip,* and *flip.* Of course there are many, many more words in these families. If you think of any others, write them on a separate sheet of paper.

WHAT'S THE WORD?

Fill in the blank with the correct word, and then circle the phonogram in the word.

1. Start with *rip*. Make it rhyme with *pig*.
   What's the word? _____

2. Start with *sit*. Make it rhyme with *tip*.
   What's the word? _____

3. Start with *pin*. Give it the same beginning sound as *fit*.
   What's the word? _____

4. Start with *dig*. Give it the same beginning sound as *win*.
   What's the word? _____

5. Start with *ten*. Give it the same vowel sound as *zip*.
   What's the word? _____

6. Start with *hat*. Give it the same vowel sound as *flip*.
   What's the word? _____

Answers on page 62.

POP QUIZ

(Hint: Answer these riddles by thinking of short i words that rhyme.)

What did the soccer player give the ball?
Answer: a quick kick

What do you call a very clever cat?
Answer: a witty kitty

Ha HA!

Ha HA!

Short o and Short u Word Families

You knew these vowels were next, didn't you? And you also know what to do now. Build word families with these phonograms. Try to come up with as many words as you can for each word family.

Words with -op	Words with -ot	Words with -ug	Words with -ut
____op	____ot	____ug	____ut
____op	____ot	____ug	____ut
____op	____ot	____ug	____ut
____op	____ot	____ug	____ut
____op	____ot	____ug	____ut
____op	____ot	____ug	____ut

Words in these families include *cop, hop, pop, top, drop, stop; dot, got, hot, knot, not, spot; bug, dug, hug, mug, tug; cut, hut, nut, rut,* and *shut.* But don't stop there! Can you think of any more words in these families?

WHERE TO PUT *PUT*?

Did you try to put the word *put* in the **-ut** word family? It looks like the other **-ut** words. But listen to its vowel sound. Does it sound like the vowel sound in *cut?* Or does it sound like the vowel sound in *look?* Usually that vowel sound is spelled **oo,** but in a few words, such as *put,* it is spelled **u.** To belong to the **-ut** word family, a word must have the short **u** sound spelled **u.**

OP, OT, UG, OR UT?

Use words from the **-op, -ot, -ug,** and **-ut** word families to finish the sentences. Then circle the phonogram in each word.

1. If it's not cold, it might be _____.
2. To _____ something, you might use a knife.
3. Now I get the paper. Yesterday I _____ the paper.
4. A _____ is a small house.
5. To _____ is to jump up and down on one foot.
6. _____ is another word for *insect.*
7. If you pull hard on the rope, you _____ it.
8. If it's not the bottom, it might be the _____.

Answers on page 62.

POP QUIZ

Riddle

One frog hopped to the dock.
Two frogs plopped into the pond.
Four frogs croaked in the bog.
How many words have short **o**?

Answer on page 62.

We Are Families

There are many other short vowel word families. But the word families presented in this chapter are some of the most common. Many of the other word families don't have as many words, but they are still useful for spelling. Watch for these word families as you read, and use them to help you when you write.

POP QUIZ

SHORT VOWEL SWITCH

Make one short vowel word into another short vowel word by changing only the vowel. Switching the vowel means the words won't be part of the same family.

1. (touch lightly) _____ ➡ (animal at home) _____ ➡
   (deep hole) _____ ➡ (something to cook in) _____

2. (light brown color) _____ ➡ (a number) _____ ➡
   (metal) _____

4. (use a key) _____ ➡ (pass your tongue over) _____ ➡
   (good fortune) _____

5. (something used to play baseball) _____ ➡ (a very small
   amount) _____ ➡ (means the same as *however*) ➡ _____

Answers on page 62.

LONG VOWEL WORD FAMILIES

Many long vowel words can be put into families, too. But, as you learned in Chapter 4, long vowel sounds can have different spellings. For example, the letter **m** and the phonogram **-ain** make the word *main*. The letter **m** and the phonogram **-ane** make the word *mane*. *Main* and *mane* sound exactly alike. So knowing what word families the words are in doesn't really help you with their spellings. What's more important is knowing what *main* and *mane* mean and when to use them. Even so, you can build a lot of words using long vowel phonograms. See how many words you can think of that have the following phonograms. (Because there aren't very many long **u** words with spelling patterns, there are no long **u** phonograms listed here.)

Words with -ake	Words with -ate	Words with -ail	Words with -ay

Words with -eak	Words with -eat	Words with -eed	Words with -eep

Words with -ide	Words with -ine	Words with -ight	Words with -y

Words with -one	Words with -oat	Words with -ow	Words with -old

Practice listening for long vowel sounds that rhyme by saying the following word pairs out loud: *base, face; made, paid; squeak, peek.* What other rhyming long vowel pairs can you think of?

DON'T BREAK YOUR BRAKES!

Words that sound alike but have different spelling and meanings, like *main* and *mane,* are called *homophones.* Here are a few long vowel words that are homophones. Be extra careful when spelling these words: Even when you have spelled a word correctly, it may be a different word than you thought you were spelling!

Long a	Long e	Long i	Long o
ate/eight	beat/beet	by/buy	know/no
bale/bail	feat/feet	I/eye	knows/nose
brake/break	heal/heel	knight/night	loan/lone
fare/fair	leak/leek	right/write	road/rode
hale/hail	meat/meet	sight/site	roll/role
grate/great	peace/piece	tied/tide	rose/rows
made/maid	peak/peek		so/sew
male/mail	read/reed		toe/tow
mane/main	real/reel		whole/hole
plane/plain	sea/see		
sale/sail	seam/seem		
tale/tail	scene/seen		
whale/wail	steal/steel		
waste/waist	weak/week		
way/weigh			
wait/weight			

mnemonic

meat or meet?
We *eat* m*ea*t.

wait or weight?
W*ait* for the tr*ai*n.

Why were the Dark Ages so dark? (Hint: Think homophones!)

Answer: They had more knights (nights) in those days.

Ha HA!

POP QUIZ ANSWERS

page 54

Word Family Sort
-am: slam, swam, jam, clam, ram; **-ap:** gap, wrap, trap, sap, chap; **-amp:** stamp, cramp, camp, lamp, ramp; **-ash:** clash, flash, mash, trash, cash

page 55

Use the Clues
1) bed, 2) ten, 3) smell, 4) men, 5) wet, 6) yell

page 57

What's the Word?
1) rig, 2) sip, 3) fin, 4) wig, 5) tin, 6) hit

page 58

op, ot, ug, or ut?
1) hot, 2) cut, 3) got, 4) hut, 5) hop, 6) bug, 7) tug, 8) top

page 59

Riddle
8 (frog, hopped, dock, frogs, plopped, pond, frogs, bog)

page 59

Short Vowel Switch
1) pat ➤ pet ➤ pit ➤ pot; 2) tan ➤ ten ➤ tin; 3) lock ➤ lick ➤ luck;
4) bat ➤ bit ➤ but

Vowel-r Sounds and Patterns
"R" You Rrrready?

Look closely at the letter **r**. It has a special power. Who knew this little letter was so powerful? The **r** uses its special power very carefully.

From Short and Long to Vowel-r

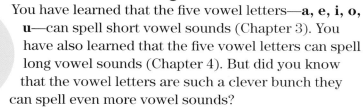

You have learned that the five vowel letters—**a, e, i, o, u**—can spell short vowel sounds (Chapter 3). You have also learned that the five vowel letters can spell long vowel sounds (Chapter 4). But did you know that the vowel letters are such a clever bunch they can spell even more vowel sounds?

Say the word *can*. What vowel sound do you hear? *Can* has the short **a** vowel sound. Now say *cane*. *Cane* has the long **a** vowel sound. Say *car*. What vowel sound do you hear? Hmmm. Is the vowel sound short? Say *can* and *car*. Do their vowel sounds sound alike? No. OK, is the vowel sound long? Say *cane* and *car*. Are their vowel sounds the same? No. Well, if the vowel sound in *car* isn't short or long, then what is it?

In the word *car*, the letter **r** after the **a** changes the vowel sound. It makes the vowel sound different than the short vowel sound or the long vowel sound that **a** usually spells.

Say the words *cot*, *coat*, and *core*. Compare the vowel sounds in these words. Which has the short **o** vowel sound? Which has the long **o** vowel sound? Which has neither? Which word has an **r** after the vowel? Aha! The letter **r** uses its special power again!

Say each picture name. Does the word have a short vowel sound, a long vowel sound, or some other vowel sound?

If you thought *ring* and *lamp* have short vowel sounds; *kite* and *rope* have long vowel sounds; and *corn* and *car* have other vowel sounds, you're right! What do you notice about the words that don't have the short or long vowel sounds? It's that sneaky little **r** again!

You already know that it's a good idea to listen carefully to the sounds in a word. They can give you clues about how to spell the word. If you see an **r** after a vowel, and the vowel sound isn't short or long, then chances are the vowel sound is a vowel-**r** sound.

Like a Star

Look at the word *star*. The **a** is followed by **r**. Say the word. The vowel sound isn't short or long. It sounds like the word *are*. Say *star* several times. You want to be able to recognize this vowel sound when you hear it.

Most words that have the vowel-**r** sound as in *star* spell the vowel sound the same way: **ar.**

Say each picture name. Circle the pictures whose names have the same vowel sound as *star.*

Barn, harp, and *yarn* have the same vowel sound as *star.* And all three of these words spell the vowel sound the same way: **ar.**

(Hint: To answer these riddles, think **ar.**)

What do you get from a bad-tempered shark?

Answer: As far away as possible!

Ha HA!

If all your clothes had been stolen, what would you go home in?

Answer: the dark

HaHA!

POP QUIZ

AR WORD PUZZLE
The answers to these clues all contain the **ar** sound.

Across

2. a building for hay and cows
3. clever
5. pointed

Down

1. piece of a whole
4. a scratch or stain made on something
6. to hurt

Answers on page 74.

Like a Horn

Look at the word *horn*. The **o** is followed by **r.** Say the word. The vowel sound isn't short or long. It sounds like the word *or.* Say *horn* several times. You want to be able to recognize this vowel sound when you hear it.

Most words that have the vowel-**r** sound as in *horn* spell the vowel sound the same way: **or.**

Say each picture name. Circle the pictures whose names have the same vowel sound as *horn*.

Fork, *corn*, and *torch* have the same vowel sound as *horn*. They are all spelled **or.**

Where did the rhino sit in the band? (Hint: Think **or**.)

Answer: the horn section

Ha HA!

A Star and a Horn

Let's review what you have learned about the vowel-**r** sounds in *star* and *horn*. When an **r** follows a vowel, the vowel sound is different than if the vowel were by itself. Say the following words out loud:

cat   pot   had   cod   ban   con

Now add an **r** after the vowel in each word, and write the new word in the space provided. Say this new word out loud. Do you hear the difference between the vowel sound (above) and the vowel-**r** sound (below)?

cat _____   had _____   ban _____

pot _____   cod _____   con _____

The following words have the same beginning and ending sounds, but they have different vowel sounds. Can you hear the difference? Hearing the difference in sounds will help you spell the words correctly.

far, for   card, cord   farm, form   part, port   barn, born   park, pork

By now you know that the more you practice, the easier it will be for you to remember the correct spellings of words. Here's a fun practice activity! Write the words *bar, jar, car, card, hard, large, dark, park, farm, start, for, fork, form, cord, more, store, corn, thorn, port,* and *sport* on index cards, one word per card. On another card, draw a star, and draw a horn on yet another card. Shuffle the word cards, and then sort the cards into piles according to which words have the vowel sound in *star* and which have the vowel sound in *horn*.

Or, read the words out loud to a partner who holds up the star card for words with the vowel sound in *star* or the horn card for words with the vowel sound in *horn*.

mnemonic

heart
He has a h*ear*t.
(Besides, a h*ar*t is a deer, d*ear*!)
four
Four has 4 letters.
hoarse
My thr*oat* is a little h*oar*se.

POP QUIZ

IS IT AR OR OR?

Write **ar** or **or** to finish the answer to each riddle.

1. What key does a hornet sing in?
   Bee sh_____p.
2. Who always goes to bed with shoes on?
   A h_____se.
3. Why do people buy things with their credit cards?
   They get a ch_____ge out of it.
4. Why are dogs like trees?
   They both have b_____ks.
5. Who is a sound sleeper?
   Someone who sn_____es.
6. Where do birds invest their money?
   In the st_____k m_____ket.

Answers on page 74.

HERE COME THE EXCEPTIONS!

The goal of a spelling book is to tell you about patterns that work for spelling lots of words. That's what makes learning patterns useful. But, as you have seen before, there are usually exceptions—other patterns that spell the same sounds.

heart   course   hoarse

Do you recognize the vowel sounds in these words? *Heart* and *star*. *Horn*, *course*, and *hoarse*. Same sounds, different spelling patterns. Don't feel discouraged—just remember, these are the exceptions. Many, many more words have the spellings **ar** and **or** for these vowel sounds. Not many words have the spellings **ear, our,** and **oar.**

Like a Bird

Say the word *bird*. The vowel sound isn't short or long. It sounds like you're saying "errr." Say *bird* several times. You want to be able to recognize this vowel sound when you hear it.

Say each picture name. Circle the pictures whose names have the same vowel sound as *bird*.

Girl, purse, and *shirt* have the same vowel sound as *bird*. As you probably noticed, there is more than one way to spell this sound. Three of the most common spellings are **ir, ur,** and **er.**

mnemonic

merge
e and **r**
"come together"
in *merge*

ER, EXCUSE ME, SIR

Practice spelling this sound by filling in the blanks. Use the clues to help you finish the words.

1. someone who works in a store   (__ __er__)

2. comes after first and second   (__ __ir__)

3. move around like a wheel   (__ur__)

4. to bring food to the table   (__ er__ __)

5. another name for mud   (__ir__)

6. get a bruise or cut   (__ur__)

Answers on page 74.

POP QUIZ

COMPLETE THE SENTENCES

Use these words to complete the sentences. Then find *all* the words that have the vowel sound in *bird*. Write those words in the correct columns in the chart.

served   nurse   whirled   shirt   hurt

1. I tripped on the curb and _____ my ankle.

2. He got dirt all over his new _____.

3. The _____ put a bandage on the boy's burn.

4. The dancer twirled and _____ across the stage.

5. Fern _____ the ball across the tennis court.

Words with the Vowel Sound in *Bird*

spelled **er**	spelled **ir**	spelled **ur**

Answers on page 74.

POP QUIZ

JUST REMEMBER THIS

There are other ways to spell the vowel sounds in *star*, *horn*, and *bird*, but **ar, or, ir, er,** and **ur** are by far the most common spellings for these sounds. That's the important thing to remember!

What's a computer's favorite sport? (Hint: Think of a word with the vowel sound in *bird*.) Answer: surfing

HaHA!

What do you call a 5,000-pound gorilla?
(Hint: To answer these riddles, think of words with the er sound.)

Answer: Sir

HaHA!

How did the bread feel when it was put in the toaster?

Answer: burned up

Ha HA!

Like a Bear

Say the word *bear*. The vowel sound isn't short or long. It isn't like the other vowel-**r** sounds you heard. It sounds like the word *air*. Say *bear* several times. You want to be able to recognize this vowel sound when you hear it.

The vowel sound you hear in *bear* can be spelled several different ways. Three of the most common are **ear,** as in *bear*; **are,** as in *share*; and **air,** as in *chair*. Say *bear, share,* and *chair*. Do you hear the same vowel sound in all three words? Yep! Once again, there's really no way to tell which spelling to use for the vowel sound. You have to memorize the correct spellings.

Say each picture name. Circle the pictures whose names have the same vowel sound as *bear*.

Square, pear, and *chair* have the same vowel sound as *bear*.

Try building word families for the **air** words by writing different consonants, consonant blends, and digraphs at the beginning. How many words can you make? If you think of more than will fit below, use a separate sheet of paper.

Words with -air		Words with -are	
_____air	_____air	_____are	_____are
_____air	_____air	_____are	_____are
_____air	_____air	_____are	_____are

Fair, hair, pair, chair, stair; care, dare, rare, ware, share, spare are just some of the words you can make. Did you think of any others? Good for you!

WORD CLUES

Fill in the blanks with **air, are,** or **ear** to finish each word so that it matches the clue.

1. to have clothes on

   w_____

2. clear and sunny

   f_____

3. not often seen

   r_____

4. strong, bright light

   gl_____

5. one step in a set

   st_____

Answers on page 74.

POP QUIZ

THE AIR UP THERE

How many **air** words can you think of that are spelled **-ear?** Probably not very many, since there are only a few: *bear, pear, tear,* and *wear* are some of them.

How can you leave the room with two legs and come back with six? (Hint: Think *air*!)

Answer: Bring a chair back with you.

Ha HA!

HOMOPHONES

Do you remember what a **homophone** is (Chapters 4 and 5)? Words that have the same sounds but different spellings and meanings are called homophones. Because the **air** vowel sound can be spelled different ways, some pairs of **air** words are homophones. For more information about homophones, see Chapter 8.

bare	bear
fare	fair
hare	hair
pare	pair
stares	stairs

mnemonic

pare/pear/pair
To p*are* or c*are*,
you use a knife.

You *eat* a p*ear*.

You and I (*i*) make
a good pa*ir*.

WHICH WORD?

Test your ability to choose the correct homophone by circling the right word.

1. Every summer my family and I go to the county fare/fair.
2. When my dog is hungry, he sits and stares/stairs at me.
3. Because she wore out her shoes, she had to buy a new pare/pair.
4. A hare/hair has longer ears than a rabbit.
5. In winter, the branches of the trees are bare/bear.

Answers on page 74.

A Star, a Horn, a Bird, and a Bear

It's time to review the vowel-**r** sounds and their spellings. Here's a quick summary:

 The vowel sound heard in *star* is most often spelled **ar** as in *star*.

The vowel sound heard in *horn* is most often spelled **or** as in *horn*.

The vowel sound heard in *bird* is most often spelled **ir** as in *bird*, **er** as in *fern*, and **ur** as in *nurse*.

The vowel sound heard in *bear* is most often spelled **air** as in *chair*, **are** as in *share*, and **ear** as in *bear*.

SPELL CHECK

Read each set of words. Circle the two words that have the same vowel-**r** sound. Write another word that has that same vowel-**r** sound *and* spelling.

1. charge, spark, perk _____
2. storm, purse, snore _____
3. nerve, stork, perch _____
4. third, skirt, card _____
5. worn, turn, curl _____

Answers on page 74.

ANSWER A RIDDLE

Use the clues to finish the words. Answer the riddle in the yellow box below by making two words out of the letters in the white boxes.

1. object in the night sky   ☐ t __ __
2. two of something   ☐ __ __ r
3. opposite of light   d ☐ __ k
4. hair on a cat   f __ ☐
5. a group of cows   h ☐ __ d
6. where a ship docks   ☐ __ __ t
7. a large furry animal   b __ ☐ __
8. an animal that flies   b __ ☐ d
9. mix with a spoon   s ☐ __ __
10. to frighten   ☐ c __ __ __

Answers on page 74.

POP QUIZ

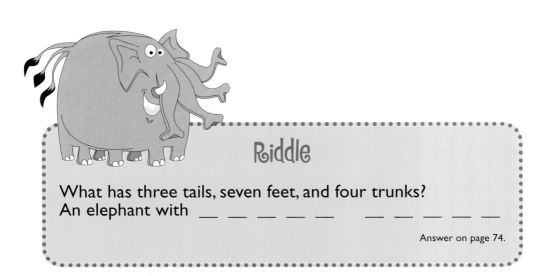

Riddle

What has three tails, seven feet, and four trunks?
An elephant with __ __ __ __ __   __ __ __ __ __

Answer on page 74.

page 65

ar Word Puzzle
Across: 2) barn, 3) smart, 5) sharp; Down: 1) part, 4) mark, 6) harm

page 67

Is It **ar** or **or**?
1) sharp, 2) horse, 3) charge, 4) barks, 5) snores, 6) stork market

page 68

Er, Excuse Me, Sir
1) clerk, 2) third, 3) turn, 4) serve, 5) dirt, 6) hurt

page 69

Complete the Sentences
1) hurt, 2) shirt, 3) nurse, 4) whirled, 5) fur
spelled **er**: Fern, served; spelled **ir**: dirt, shirt, twirled, whirled; spelled **ur**: curb, hurt, nurse, burn

page 71

Word Clues
1) wear, 2) fair, 3) rare, 4) glare, 5) stair

page 72

Which Word?
1) fair, 2) stares, 3) pair, 4) hare, 5) bare

page 72

Spell Check
1) charge and spark—possible word: yard, 2) storm and snore—possible word: short,
3) nerve and perch—possible word: clerk, 4) third and skirt—possible word: dirt,
5) turn and curl—possible word: hurt

page 73

Answer a Riddle
1) star, 2) pair, 3) dark, 4) fur, 5) herd, 6) port, 7) bear, 8) bird, 9) stir, 10) scare
Riddle answer: spare parts

Other Vowel Sounds
Enjoy the Power

Here come the vowels again! And they are still making new sounds. They say "ow!" They say "oy!" They say "uh!" They work together, they work alone, and they work with y and **w**. Vowels, as you have already seen, are very versatile.

The Long, the Short, and the Vowel-r's

Say these words out loud. What vowel sound do you hear in each word?

cat	hen	pig	fox	bug
cake	leaf	five	boat	cube
star	horn	bird	bear	

Which have short vowel sounds?

_____
_____
_____
_____
_____

Which have long vowel sounds?

_____
_____
_____
_____
_____

Which have vowel-r sounds?

_____
_____
_____
_____

You should be a pro at this by now! *Cat, hen, pig, fox,* and *bug* have short vowel sounds; *cake, leaf, five, boat,* and *cube* have long vowel sounds; and *star, horn, bird,* and *bear* have vowel-**r** sounds. Good for you!

Now what about these words? What vowel sounds do you hear in them?

mouse   cow   boy   coin

Hmmm. Are the vowel sounds short? Are they long? Are they vowel-**r** sounds? No, no, and no. They are two new vowel sounds, and you're about to meet them.

The Mouse and the Cow

Say the words *mouse* and *cow*. Do they have the same vowel sound? Why, yes, they do. This vowel sound (which is also heard in *vowel* and *sound*, by the way) sounds like "ow." Maybe someone pulled the mouse's tail! Maybe someone poked the cow! So the mouse and the cow said, "OW!"

Say the following words out loud, and circle the ones that contain the vowel sound you hear in *mouse* and *cow*.

south	drove	truck	value
stop	huge	pound	throat
clown	bunch	knock	how
stroll	spout	growl	menu

Did you circle *south*, *clown*, *spout*, *pound*, *growl*, and *how*? Listen carefully to hear the "ow" sound in each of these words. What do you notice about the words you circled? They have the same vowel sound—but not the same spelling for the vowel sound. It's spelled **ou** in some words and **ow** in other words.

Same vowel sound, but two different spellings. Well, no big surprise there, right? You figured out a long time ago that the English language is filled with exceptions and variations. Remember how many ways there are to spell long **a?** There's **a–e, ai, ay, ei, ea,** and **ey.** And what about long **e?** Long **e** can be spelled **ee, ea, e, ie,** and **ei.** So with just two ways to spell "ow," it almost seems like you're getting off easy, doesn't it?

So the "ow" vowel sound can be spelled **ou** or **ow.** But when does each spelling appear? Remember this hint when figuring out which spelling is correct: **ou** never appears at the end of words, while **ow** can appear at the end. (But, of course, **ow** at the end doesn't have to spell the "ow" sound. Look at *crow* and *grow,* for example.)

OPPOSITES QUIZ

Fill in the blanks with the **ou** or **ow** word that is the opposite of the underlined word.

1. not <u>north</u>, but _____

2. not <u>up</u>, but _____

3. not <u>then</u>, but _____

4. not <u>smile</u>, but _____

5. not <u>in</u>, but _____

6. not <u>lost</u>, but _____

Answers on page 84.

POP QUIZ

HAVEN'T WE MET BEFORE?

Yes, you have seen the **ow** pattern before. Do you remember where? In the long **o** patterns (Chapter 4). The letters **ow** can spell the long **o** sound. They can also spell the "ow" sound. Think about *bow* (rhymes with *snow*) and *bow* (rhymes with *cow*). Same letters, same beginning sounds, two different vowel sounds, two different meanings. And to say the word correctly, you just have to know which meaning is being used.

The gift has a bow on it.

Does that bow have the long **o** or "ow" sound?

He took a bow after singing his song.

How about that one?

Knock, knock!
Who's there?
Howard.
Howard who?
Howard you like to be outside for a change?
Ha HA! HaHA!

The Boy with the Coins

Say the words *coins* and *boy*. Do they have the same vowel sound? Oy, they do. The vowel sound sounds like "oy." Maybe the boy got a lot of gold coins. He was so excited that he said, "Oh, boy!"

Say the following words out loud, and circle the ones that have the same vowel sound heard in *coins* and *boy*.

joint	close	chain	voice
gold	coach	enjoy	groan
clock	toil	pond	toy
annoy	spray	thrown	toes

What do you notice about the words you circled (*joint, annoy, toil, enjoy, voice,* and *toy*)? They all have the same vowel sound, but they have different spellings for the vowel sound.

Same vowel sound, two different spellings. Remember long **o** from Chapter 4? How many patterns did you learn that can spell long **o**? There's **o, o–e, oa, ow, oe,** and **o** followed by **ld, ll, lt,** and **st.** Whew!

The "oy" vowel sound can be spelled **oi** or **oy**. And once again there's really no way to tell which spelling to use . . . except for this clue: **oi** doesn't appear at the end of words, while **oy** can appear at the end.

But here's good news: Unlike other vowel combinations, **oi** and **oy** don't spell any other sounds. They spell the "oy" sound only.

Build Words

This activity will help you remember which "oy" words have which spelling. Write the consonants **b, c, f, j, s,** and **t** on index cards, one letter per card. Do the same for the consonant blends **br** and **sp.** Next, write the word patterns __**oy** and __**oil** at the top of two columns on a sheet of paper. Place each letter card at the beginning of each word pattern. See how many words you can make by combining a consonant or consonant blend with each word pattern. Write the words below the word patterns.

POP QUIZ

WHAT'S THE WORD?

Write the **oi** or **oy** word that goes with each clue.

1. another word for dirt _____
2. the opposite of *girl* _____
3. to link together _____
4. something children play with _____
5. sharp end of a pencil _____
6. another word for happiness _____

Answers on page 84.

Knock, knock!

Who's there?

Ya.

Ya who?

I didn't know you were a **cowboy**!

HaHA!

MAKE A CHOICE

Complete the sentences using the **oi** and **oy** words below.

choice   noise   loyal   annoy   enjoy   voice

1. The neighbor's dog makes a lot of _____.

   That dog is starting to _____ me!

2. Anya has a lovely _____.

   I _____ listening to her sing.

3. Potatoes are usually my family's _____ for dinner.

   We are very _____ to that vegetable.

Answers on page 84.

POP QUIZ

What happens when you pamper a cow?
(Hint: Think "oy"!)

Answer: You get spoiled milk.

Ha HA!

The Mouse, the Cow, the Boy, and the Coins

You know that the "ow" vowel sound can be spelled **ou** as in *mouse* or **ow** as in *cow*. And you know the "oy" vowel sound is spelled **oi** as in *coins* or **oy** as in *boy*. It's time to review. One good way to do this is to look for these words in the books and magazines you read. For practice, ask Mom or Dad if you can take a page from a newspaper or magazine and look for words that have the "ow" vowel sound. Circle these words in red pencil or pen. Now look for words that have the "oy" vowel sound. Circle those words in green pencil or pen. Then write down all the words you found, writing them in groups based on their vowel sounds and spelling. Count the words in each list. Which vowel sound did you find most often? Which spelling was the most common?

Write Tongue Twisters

Another way to practice spelling these sounds is to try writing a tongue twister with "ow" or "oy" words. The trick is to use as many "ow" or "oy" words as possible and also to use as many similar-sounding (or rhyming) words as possible. Remember: Tongue twisters are meant to be silly, and they don't even need to make sense! They are just supposed to be difficult to say.
Here are two examples:

Cows bow down to clowns in gowns.

An oyster met an oyster,
And they were oysters two;
Two oysters met two oysters,
And they were oysters, too;
Four oysters met a pint of milk,
And they were oyster stew.

POP QUIZ

SPELL CHECK

Read each set of words, and decide which two words have the same vowel sound. Write another word that has that same vowel sound *and* spelling.

1. couch	house	hose	_____
2. boil	bounce	voice	_____
3. flown	how	frown	_____
4. boy	bow	enjoy	_____
5. foil	found	mouth	_____
6. broil	bowl	joint	_____

Answers on page 84.

RHYME TIME

Complete each rhyme. Write an **ow** or **oy** word that rhymes with each under-lined word.

1. It's a very tiny <u>house.</u> The right size for a _____.

2. It was his favorite <u>toy</u> when he was a _____.

3. Before you put meat in to <u>broil,</u> you must wrap it in _____.

4. The treasure she <u>found</u> was buried in the _____.

5. Without a <u>doubt,</u> I know what that book is _____.

Answers on page 84.

POP QUIZ

What's a Schwa?

Schwa. What's that? Something to eat? A new dance? Or maybe it's the sound your corduroy pants make?

Nope—none of the above, but a schwa does have something to do with sound. A schwa is a symbol that stands for . . . the "schwa" sound. Say the word *ahead.* Do you hear the vowel sound at the beginning? It sounds like "uh." That's the schwa sound.

The schwa sound is the most common vowel sound in English. But you won't hear it in words with one syllable. A **syllable** is any part of a word that has a vowel sound (see Chapter 9). That is, a word has one syllable for every vowel sound it has. It's not the number of vowel *letters* that tells you the number of syllables;

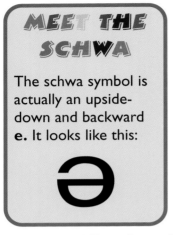

MEET THE SCHWA

The schwa symbol is actually an upside-down and backward **e.** It looks like this:

ə

it's the number of vowel *sounds*. As you know by now, two vowel letters can stand for one vowel sound. (Of course, sounds are made differently in different dialects, and that's okay!) *Dialect* is the way different people pronounce the same word.

The word *cabin* contains the vowels **a** and **i**. What vowel sound does the **a** stand for? Short **a.** What vowel sound does the **i** stand for? The schwa sound. So *cabin* has two vowel sounds. How many syllables does it have? Two. One syllable for each vowel sound.

Schwa Sounds

The schwa sound can be a bit trickier than the other vowel sounds. To practice recognizing it, say each word out loud. Then fill in the chart.

	Number of Vowel Sounds	Does It Have a Schwa Sound?
kitten	_____	_____
nine	_____	_____
muffin	_____	_____
boat	_____	_____
dragon	_____	_____

Kitten, muffin, and *dragon* each have two vowel sounds and two syllables. *Nine* and *boat* each have one. Notice that there is no schwa sound in the one-syllable words, but there is in the two-syllable words. Generally, when a word has two or more vowel sounds, at least one of them is the schwa sound—depending on dialect.

mnemonic

angel
An*gel* is soft as *gel*.

angle
An*gle* is hard as *gle*aming steel.

WHAT LETTERS SPELL THE SCHWA SOUND?

All five vowel letters—**a, e, i, o,** and **u**—can spell the schwa sound. It's true!
Say each of these words out loud. Can you hear which letter spells the schwa
sound in each word?

medal: The **a** spells the schwa sound.   *happen:* The **e** spells the schwa sound.

basin: The **i** spells the schwa sound.   *bacon:* The **o** spells the schwa sound.

census: The **u** spells the schwa sound.

mnemonic

metal vs. medal
Remember, *t*in is in me*t*al.
You wear a me*d*al like a ba*d*ge.

WHAT'S THE WORD?

Fill in the blanks with the correct word, and then circle the vowel that spells
the schwa sound in the word.

1. a plant that grows in the desert   _____

2. another word for a couch   _____

3. a coin worth five cents   _____

4. another word for *student*   _____

5. the opposite of the top   _____

6. an animal with one or two humps   _____

Answers on page 84.

POP QUIZ

(Hint: Think schwa sound!)
What has the head of a cat and the tail of a cat but isn't a cat?
Answer: a kitten
Ha HA!

POP QUIZ ANSWERS

page 77

Opposites Quiz
1) south, 2) down, 3) now, 4) frown, 5) out, 6) found

page 79

What's the Word?
1) soil, 2) boy, 3) join, 4) toy, 5) point, 6) joy

page 79

Make a Choice
1) noise, annoy; 2) voice, enjoy; 3) choice, loyal

page 81

Spell Check
1) couch and house—possible word: shout, 2) boil and voice— possible word: noise, 3) how and frown—possible word: clown, 4) boy and enjoy— possible word: toy, 5) found and mouth—possible word: count, 6) broil and joint—possible word: toil

page 81

Rhyme Time
1) mouse, 2) boy, 3) foil, 4) ground, 5) about

page 83

What's the Word?
1) cactus, 2) sofa, 3) nickel, 4) pupil, 5) bottom, 6) camel

Plurals, Contractions, and Compounds
Be a Word Builder

Words are like building blocks. You can add letters to them or take letters away to make new forms of words. You can even join words together to make new words. But don't be fooled by words that look and sound like other words!

More than One

Nouns that name one person, place, or thing are **singular.** Nouns that name more than one person, place, or thing are **plural.** To make the plural of most nouns, add **s.**

dog ➡ *dogs*   *boy* ➡ *boys*   *game* ➡ *games*

But that's not all there is to making plurals. There are many exceptions to the main rule. You'll need to learn these exceptions to spell the plurals of all words correctly. These are the exceptions:

✓ Nouns ending in **s, ss, ch, sh, x,** or **zz**: Add **es** to form the plural.

gas ➡ *gases*   *class* ➡ *classes*   *church* ➡ *churches*   *fox* ➡ *foxes*
buzz ➡ *buzzes*

✓ Nouns ending with a consonant and **y**: Change the **y** to **i** and add **es** to form the plural.

baby ➡ *babies*   *fly* ➡ *flies*   *penny* ➡ *pennies*   *country* ➡ *countries*

✓ Some nouns ending in **f** or **fe**: Change the **f** or **fe** to *v* and add **es** to form the plural.

elf ➡ *elves*   *half* ➡ *halves*   *life* ➡ *lives*   *self* ➡ *selves*

However, most nouns that end in **f** or **fe** form the plural in the usual way, by adding **s.**

✔ Some nouns ending with a consonant and **o**: Add **es** to form the plural.

echo ➡ *echoes*   *hero* ➡ *heroes*   *potato* ➡ *potatoes*

A fun fact to remember is that music words that end in a consonant followed by **o** add **s** to form the plural (as in *piano* ➡ *pianos*).

✔ Most nouns ending with a vowel and **o**: Add **s** to form the plural.

radio ➡ *radios*   *video* ➡ *videos*   *rodeo* ➡ *rodeos*

✔ Some nouns have **irregular** plurals:

man ➡ *men*   *mouse* ➡ *mice*   *child* ➡ *children*   *tooth* ➡ *teeth*

✔ A few nouns spell the plural and the singular the same way. These are generally the names of fish, birds, and mammals:

sheep ➡ *sheep*   *deer* ➡ *deer*   *fish* ➡ *fish*

PERFECTING PLURALS

This poet needs some help in spelling plurals. Now that you know all the rules, can you come to the rescue? Fix the plural words so they are spelled correctly.

All childs make wishiz,
as many as fishs
that swim in the seaz,
or leafies that blow in the breeze,
wishiz for toyes and noise
and favorite dishis.

Answers on page 99.

POP QUIZ

Where do kings keep their armies? (Hint: Think plurals.)

Answer: up their sleevies

Ha HA!

POP QUIZ

PLURAL POWER

Complete each sentence by writing the plural form of the noun in parentheses ( ).

Sometimes you need to put your _____ (belief) into actions.

Our class heard about poor _____ (person) in Africa.

We wanted to send them _____ (box) of food and clothes.

We could not send foods such as milk and _____ (potato)

because they would spoil. Canned _____ (good) would be

heavy and expensive to send. We decided to gather _____

(dress), shirts, and jeans. We also had a few bake _____ (sale)

to raise money. With that money we were able to buy socks and

_____ (shoe). Lots of other _____ (child) joined our

drive. We were so proud of _____ (ourself) for raising $500!

Answers on page 99.

Shrinking Words

You may not realize it, but you and your friends use short forms for many words when you talk. These short forms are called **contractions**—two words with one or more letters left out joined together to make one word. An apostrophe shows where the letter(s) have been left out.

Maybe you've had a conversation like this one:

"How'd you like to get a pizza?"

"Let's get pepperoni. I can't stand mushrooms!"

"Ugh. Don't order peppers on it!"

In those few sentences, you and your friends have used four contractions. Can you find them? (The contractions are *how'd*, *let's*, *can't*, and *don't*.)

To spell a contraction correctly, be sure to:

1. Join the words.

2. Leave out the correct letters.

3. Put the apostrophe where the letters should be.

The following table shows many common contractions.

Contraction	Formed from	Contraction	Formed from
I'm	I am	isn't	is not
you're	you are	aren't	are not
it's	it is	wasn't	was not
we're	we are	can't	cannot
they're	they are	don't	do not
I've	I have	didn't	did not
you've	you have	doesn't	does not
she'd	she had, she would	hasn't	has not
we'll	we will	haven't	have not
who's	who is, who has	won't	will not
you'd	you had, you would	would've	would have
I'd	I had, I would	should've	should have

YOU DO NOT SAY

People came up with contractions to save time in speaking and writing. Shortcuts such as *don't* and *can't* were introduced hundreds of years ago—in about 1642, as a matter of fact. However, back then, using contractions was considered sloppy speech! Can you imagine trying to talk to your friends today without using contractions?

Do you think it is going to rain today?

No, I do not think it is going to rain today.

Pop Quiz

TRY IT! YOU'LL LIKE IT!

There are 12 places in this story in which you can replace two words with a contraction. Can you find them all? Circle the words, and write the contractions in the blanks provided. Be careful where you place the apostrophes!

Adam does not like to try new foods. He is not one bit adventurous when it comes to food. Aunt Mary said she would get him to try something wild.

"That is never going to happen!" Adam declared.

"We will have to wait and see," replied Aunt Mary. That night she placed a platter of "fried crunchies" on the table.

"What is this?" Adam asked. "Do not you have potato chips instead?"

"It is something I like to call 'fried crunchies,'" Aunt Mary said. "They are a delicacy eaten by Asian kings."

"Kings eat these? I will try one," he said. He popped one into his mouth. "Wow! It is delicious!" he said.

Before he knew it, he had eaten a whole plate of vegetables fried in a tempura batter. Aunt Mary smiled and raised her arms in victory.

_____ _____ _____ _____

_____ _____ _____ _____

_____ _____ _____ _____

Answers on page 99.

Compound Words

Is a *butterfly* a fly made of butter or a stick of butter that flies? Does your head get soaked during a *brainstorm?* If you ate a *firecracker,* would it burn your tongue?

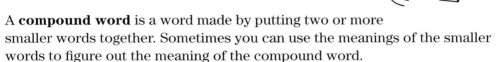

As you'll see, in a compound word one plus one doesn't always equal two!

A **compound word** is a word made by putting two or more smaller words together. Sometimes you can use the meanings of the smaller words to figure out the meaning of the compound word.

doghouse	(dog + house)	A doghouse is a house for a dog.
haystack	(hay + stack)	A haystack is a stack made of hay.
classroom	(class + room)	A classroom is a room for classes.

Sometimes the meaning of the compound word is very different from the meanings of the two smaller words. For example, a *honeymoon* is not a moon made of honey! It is a trip for newlyweds. A *seesaw* is not a saw that you see! It is a piece of playground equipment made from a board and a center support. Sometimes you need a dictionary to learn the meaning of a compound word.

However, you can make a compound word easier to spell by breaking it into its parts. Compound words may be formed in three ways:

All One Word	**Joined with Hyphens**	**Separate Words**
schoolbook	good-hearted	dump truck
football	father-in-law	ice cream
highway	merry-go-round	outer space

(Hint: Think of a compound word.)
What goes through a door but never comes in or goes out?
Answer: a keyhole
Ha HA!

COMPOUNDS IN THE COUNTRY

Circle all the compound words in the story. (Hint: You should find 18.)

Molly Mosquito flew southwest along the highway. She was on her way to visit her friend Harold, a housefly who lived on a farm. She admired the countryside around her. She watched for the landmark Harold had told her about—a scarecrow standing next to a big haystack.

A sudden cloudburst forced her to take shelter under an overpass. "Whew! That was close!" she said. After the rain ended, she asked a good-natured dragonfly about the directions.

"Oh, yes, you can't miss it," he said. Off Molly flew! With a tailwind behind her, she covered the miles in a heartbeat.

Harold was standing in the doorway of his farmhouse, waving. "Come in, come in!" he cried. "I'm thrilled to see you!" He led Molly into the dining room and served his favorite treat—catfish ice cream!

Answers on page 100.

POP QUIZ

Possessives ('s, s')

A **possessive** noun shows ownership. To do that, it needs an apostrophe (').
Many people have a hard time with apostrophes. Are you one of these people?
Take a look at the following sentences.

My friend's ride the bus.   My friends ride is boring.

Both are wrong. If you're not sure why the apostrophe is placed incorrectly, or if you're not sure if an apostrophe is missing, read on!

A singular noun forms the possessive by adding **'s.**

Dennis**'s** books   (The books belong to one person: Dennis.)

a dog**'s** kennel   (One dog lives in the kennel.)

a fly**'s** buzzing   (One fly is making a buzzing sound.)

✓ A plural noun that ends in **s** forms the possessive by adding only an apostrophe (').

two boys' books	(The books belong to two people.)
the dogs' kennel	(Two or more dogs live in the kennel.)
the flies' buzzing	(Two or more flies are buzzing.)

WATCH IT!

Be careful where you put the apostrophe! If you slip up by one letter, you may change the meaning of the possessive. *The cat's food* means food belonging to one cat. *The cats' food* means food belonging to two or more cats.

✓ You probably remember that not all plural nouns end in **s**. Plural nouns that do not end in **s** form the possessive by adding **'s**.

the children's idea	(Two or more children have an idea.)
the feet's comfort	(Both feet—or feet in general—feel comfortable.)

Now that you know the rules, look again at these apostrophe challenge sentences.

My friend's ride the bus.

Is the word *friends* showing ownership? No. It is the subject of the sentence. Who rides? Friends ride. So *friends* is simply a plural noun. It should not have an apostrophe. The sentence should read:

My friends ride the bus.

What about the second sentence?

My friends ride is boring.

Is the word *friends* showing ownership? Yes. It tells whose ride. So it should have an apostrophe (') or an apostrophe and an **s** ('**s**). Which should it be? The first sentence told you that there are two or more friends riding the bus. So the possessive in the second sentence is a plural possessive. To form a plural possessive, add **'**. The sentence should read:

My friends' ride is boring.

POSSESSIVE PRONOUN OR CONTRACTION?

Possessive pronouns do not need an apostrophe.

your life   whose CD

The problem is theirs.   The pleasure is ours.

Contractions, though, do need an apostrophe.

Who's going to the mall? *Who's* is the contraction for *who is.*

You're bigger than he is.   *You're* is the contraction for *you are.*

POP QUIZ

SCHOOL BUS BLUES

Read this story, and circle all the incorrect possessive nouns. Write them correctly on another sheet of paper, adding **'** or **'s** as needed and removing apostrophes that do not belong.

The bus' driver is nice but strict. "Stay in your seat or stay off the bus," he says. "The choice is yours'." The bus heating and cooling systems are reversed so that riders' freeze in winter and burn up in summer. I am not saying the seats are uncomfortable, but some seats springs have sprung. And what about the smells of gym shoe's and old lunches? I like Sams suggestion, which is to get a bus with treat's and movies. A luxury van with a TV is Carol's idea—even better!

Answers on page 100.

Look-alikes and Soundalikes

Can a king rain for 40 years? Does a bell peel because it is sunburned? Some words are tricky because they sound or look alike.

LOOK-ALIKE WORDS

What does the word *bass* mean? That depends. There are two words with this spelling. One is a type of fish. The other is a deep voice or instrument. To know which word is meant, you have to look at how it is used.

We caught five bass in the lake.

Uncle Ron sings bass in the choir.

Words that are spelled the same but have different meanings are called **homographs.** *Homograph* means "written (*graph*) the same (*homo*)." An example of a homograph is the word *bank*. Look up *bank* in a dictionary. Do you see two entries? One kind of bank is a business that deals in money. The other kind of bank is the ridge of land along a river. Although you may know the spelling, you must check the context to be sure of the meaning.

Homographs often sound the same. For example, look up *fair* in a dictionary. The word meaning "just" or "honest" sounds the same as the word meaning "an exhibition of goods or products." However, some homographs have different pronunciations. Here are a few examples:

desert (DEH-zurt) *noun* a dry place
(di-ZURT) *verb* to abandon

minute (MIN-uht) *noun* 60 seconds
(my-NOOT) *adjective* tiny

present (PREZ-ent) *noun* a gift
(prih-ZENT) *verb* to give

wind (WIND) *noun* a current of air
(WYND) *verb* to coil or pass around something

wound (WOOND) *noun* injury
(WOWND) *verb* past tense of *wind*

NOT IDENTICAL TWINS!

Choose homographs from the word bank to complete each sentence. (Note: You will not use all the words in the word bank.)

sow/sow	wound/wound	present/present	wind/wind
lead/lead	minute/minute	desert/desert	

1. The nurse _____ a bandage around the _____.
2. I'd like to _____ this _____ to the birthday girl.
3. The captain can _____ if he will get the _____ out.
4. The troops will not _____ in the _____.
5. Feed the _____ after you _____ those seeds.

Answers on page 100.

What is the difference between a train and a tree?

Answer: One leaves its shed, and the other sheds its leaves.

HaHA!

SOUNDALIKE WORDS

Some words sound alike but are spelled differently and have different meanings. You place an *ad* in the paper, but you *add* two numbers. You might go around in a *daze* for several *days* if you win the lottery. **Homophones** are words that sound the same but are spelled differently. *Homophone* means "same sound."

Learn the spellings and meanings of homophones. Then you will not confuse them. Study this list of common homophones:

Common Homophones			
ant/aunt	blew/blue	fair/fare	groan/grown
ball/bawl	buy/by/bye	feat/feet	hair/hare
bare/bear	cent/scent/sent	flour/flower	hear/here
be/bee	chili/chilly	four/for/fore	heard/herd
beat/beet	days/daze	gnu/knew/new	knows/nose

(continued)

Common Homophones *(continued)*			
mail/male	read/red	son/sun	their/there/they're
main/mane	real/reel	stair/stare	threw/through
pail/pale	right/write	tacks/tax	throne/thrown
pair/pare/pear	sew/so/sow	tail/tale	to/too/two
pause/paws	some/sum	tea/tee	way/weigh

capitol
A capitol has a dome.

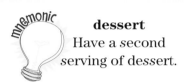

dessert
Have a second
serving of dessert.

HOMOPHONES FOR SALE/SAIL

Choose the correct homophone to complete each sentence.

You can't _____ (beat/beet) our prices! This is the best _____ (buy/by) in town, with the best prices you'll ever _____ (sea/see). You'll stop. You'll _____ (stair/stare). You won't believe _____ (your/you're) eyes! Don't let this opportunity go to _____ (waist/waste). Friday _____ (morning/mourning) only, there will be no sales _____ (tacks/tax) on your purchase. Check out our perfume counter. Every _____ (cent/scent/sent) has a heavenly price. We must _____ (cell/sell) everything! We've _____ (throne/thrown) caution to the wind!

Don't delay! This sale lasts one _____ (weak/week) only. Look for the _____ (read/red) tags to find _____ (real/reel) bargains.

Answers on page 100.

POP QUIZ

Sail for Sale

What color is the wind? (Hint: Think homophones!)

HaHA!

Answer: blew (blue)

Ha HA!

What animal do you look like in the bath?

Answer: a little bare (bear)

Dr. Sr.:
Pls. sd. me yr.
12-in. model pln.
I lk. frwd. to
hrng. fr. you.

Short and Sweet

This writer wanted to save time and space. So she shortened many of her words by leaving out the vowels. She definitely overdid it, but we often do shorten words by combining them or leaving out some of their letters. Contractions are just one example. Here are some others.

ABBREVIATIONS

Abbreviations are shortened forms of words. Most abbreviated words are followed by a period. Here are some types of words that are often abbreviated:

Titles
Mr. (mister)
Jr., Sr. (junior, senior)
Sen. (senator)
Rev. (reverend)
Dr. (doctor)
M.D. (medical doctor)

Units of measurement

ft. (feet)	m (meters)
in. (inches)	cm (centimeters)
yd. (yards)	km (kilometers)
mi. (miles)	g (grams)
lbs. (pounds)	ml (milliliters)
oz. (ounces)	l (liters)
c. (cups)	
qt. (quarts)	
gal. (gallons)	

MAKING A STATEMENT

When you write a state abbreviation on an envelope, use the postal code. This is a two-letter abbreviation with no periods. For example, the postal codes for states beginning with A are:

AL   Alabama
AK   Alaska
AZ   Arizona
AR   Arkansas

What state do you live in? What is its postal code?

Time words

A.D. (*anno Domini*, "in the year of the Lord")

B.C. (before Christ) or B.C.E (before the common era)

A.M. (*ante meridiem*, "before noon")

P.M. (*post meridiem*, "after noon")

Mon., Tues., Wed., Thurs., Fri., Sat., Sun.

Jan., Feb., Mar., Apr., Jun., Jul., Aug., Sept., Oct., Nov., Dec.

Other words

Some abbreviations are formed from the first letters of the words in a name. They are spelled with all capitals and no periods. We say each letter in these abbreviations.

YMCA (Young Men's Christian Association)

IRS (Internal Revenue Service)

ABC (American Broadcasting Company)

FBI (Federal Bureau of Investigation)

TV (television)

CD (compact disc)

CD-ROM (compact disc–read-only memory)

VCR (videocassette recorder)

ACRONYMS

Sometimes we say the letters in an abbreviation as though they are a word. These abbreviations are called **acronyms.** NASCAR (National Association for Stock Car Auto Racing), NASA (National Aeronautics and Space Administration), and SWAT (Special Weapons and Tactics) are examples of acronyms.

BLENDS

Sometimes new words are created by putting parts of two or more words together. These are called **blends.** Motel (*mo*tor + h*otel*) and brunch (*br*eakfast + l*unch*) are examples of blends.

BLEND-O-RAMA

Match each blended word with the words that were used to form it.

1. telethon
2. twirl
3. squiggle
4. splatter
5. motorcade

a. motor + cavalcade
b. television + marathon
c. splash + spatter
d. twist + whirl
e. squirm + wiggle

Answers on page 100.

POP QUIZ

POP QUIZ ANSWERS

page 86

Perfecting Plurals

Word	Rule
children	Some nouns have irregular plurals.
wishes	Nouns ending in **sh** add **es**.
fish	The plural of some nouns is spelled the same way as the singular.
seas	Most nouns add **s**.
leaves	For some nouns ending in **f**, change the **f** to **v** and add **es**.
wishes	Nouns ending in **sh** add **es**.
toys	Most nouns add **s**.
dishes	Nouns ending in **sh** add **es**.

page 87

Plural Power

beliefs, people, boxes, potatoes, goods, dresses, sales, shoes, children, ourselves

page 89

Try It! You'll Like It!

doesn't, isn't, She'd, That's, We'll, What's, Don't, It's, They're, I'll, It's, he'd

page 91

Compounds in the Country
southwest, highway, housefly, countryside, landmark, scarecrow, haystack, cloudburst, overpass, good-natured, dragonfly, tailwind, heartbeat, doorway, farmhouse, dining room, catfish, ice cream

page 93

School Bus Blues
The bus driver is nice but strict. "Stay in your seat or stay off the bus," he says. "The choice is yours." The bus's heat and cooling systems are reversed so that riders freeze in winter and burn up in summer. I am not saying the seats are uncomfortable, but some seats' springs have sprung. And what about the smells of gym shoes and old lunches? I like Sam's suggestion, which is to get a bus with treats and movies. A luxury van with a TV is Carol's idea—even better!

page 95

Not Identical Twins!
1) wound/wound, 2) present/present, 3) lead/lead, 4) desert/desert, 5) sow/sow

page 96

Homophones for Sale/Sail
beat, buy, see, stare, your, waste, morning, tax, scent, sell, thrown, week, red, real

page 99

Blend-o-Rama
1) b, 2) d, 3) e, 4) c, 5) a

Working with Syllables
How to Handle Big Words

Short, simple words may be easy to read and spell, but you can challenge yourself with big words, too!

We will go to school with you.

All the words in that sentence are short and simple. That makes them easy to read—and to spell. It also makes the sentence a bit dull. Fortunately, there are lots of words that can make sentences more interesting. Unfortunately, bigger words can be harder to learn. (What did you do to help you read *fortunately, interesting,* and *unfortunately?* Did you break them down into their parts?) If you're having trouble reading or spelling a word, try breaking it into **syllables.**

What's a Syllable?

A **syllable** is any part of a word that has a vowel sound. That is, a word has one vowel sound for every syllable.

To find the number of syllables in a word:

1. Say the word.

2. Decide how many vowel sounds you hear.

3. Remember to count vowel pairs that stand for one sound as one vowel sound. For example, the **oi** in *coin,* the **ou** in *house,* the **ea** in *break,* or the **ai** in *main:* Each are two vowel letters, but just one vowel sound.

4. Remember that some vowel letters do not stand for sounds at all. For example, the **e** in *made* is silent.

5. The number of vowel sounds tells you the number of syllables.

For example, the word *outside* has two vowel sounds. The **ou** vowel pair stands for the "ow" sound, the **i** stands for the long **i** sound, and the final **e** is silent. So *outside* has two syllables.

There are four main rules for dividing words into syllables. Read on to find out what they are!

How Many Syllables?

Count the vowel sounds to find the number of syllables in each word. Write the number in the blank next to the word.

shout _____   riddle _____   ticket _____

late _____   responsible _____   umbrella _____

impossible _____   kitchen _____   steak _____

wheelbarrow _____   sheep _____   hunger _____

boy _____   supermarket _____   pepper _____

parade _____   deliver _____   necessary _____

frown _____   kangaroo _____   peanut _____

Answers on page 108.

POP QUIZ

Dividing Doubles

A pond setting.

Water like a mirror.

Threw a pebble in the shallows.

Made a ripple in the middle.

Curious minnow came to nibble.

This poet used lots of words that have one thing in common. Do you see what it is? The words have double consonants in the middle.

Rule 1 for dividing words into syllables: If a word has two like consonants in the middle, it is divided between the two consonants.

(Hint: Think double-consonant words.)

What turns everything around but doesn't move?

Answer: a mirror.

HaHA!

ham **mer**

DOUBLE DIVIDE

Divide each word into syllables with a slash mark (/).

puppet	mitten
funny	cabbage
jogger	buzzard
merry	suppose
happy	office
mirror	blizzard
error	bullet
sorry	pepper
rabbit	shallow
button	common

Answers on page 108.

POP QUIZ

(Hint: Think double-consonant words.)

What do you call two bananas?

Answer: a pair of slippers

Ha HA!

Middle but Not Matching

Words such as *corner*, *cartoon*, and *early* have two different consonants in the middle, but they have something in common with words such as *middle* and *common*.

✓ Rule 2 for dividing words into syllables: If a word has two unlike consonants in the middle, it is divided between the two consonants.

Take the words *bas/ket*, *pen/cil*, *pic/ture*, and *win/dow*, for example.

CONSONANT PAIRS THAT STICK TOGETHER

Do not split up consonant digraphs such as **ch, th, ph, sh,** and **wh.** Remember, they stand for one consonant sound, so treat them as one consonant when you are dividing words.

or/chard   mar/shal   go/pher   gath/er

What pet makes the loudest noise?
Answer: a trum-pet
Ha HA!

TWO-SYLLABLE SHUFFLE

Circle the word in each group that has two syllables.
Divide that word into syllables with a slash mark (/).

1. Making music: trumpet   flute   piano
2. On the table: plate   napkin   glass
3. Things with wings: insect   bird   bat
4. Times of day: morning   noon   night
5. Health helpers: dentist   nurse   pharmacist
6. Body parts: arms   heart   fingers
7. In the bathroom: soap   tub   shampoo
8. In court: lawyer   judge   defendant
9. Fun times: games   party   sleepover
10. Keeping warm: blanket   gloves   coat

Answers on page 108.

What did the skeleton play in the band?
Answer: a trom-bone
HaHA!

POP QUIZ

The Lone Consonant

A *lilac* and a *lily* are both flowers. Both begin with *l–i–l*. But take a closer look. What is the first vowel sound in each word? How would you divide each word into syllables?

✓ **Rule 3 for dividing words into syllables:** If a word has a single consonant in the middle, it is divided before or after the consonant, depending on whether the vowel is long or short.

• If the first vowel sound is *long,* divide *before* the consonant.

li/lac   ti/ger   mu/sic   ho/tel

• If the first vowel sound is *short,* divide *after* the consonant.

lil/y   col/or   lem/on   phon/ics

lilac   *lily*

mnemonic

busy
Busy us.

THE ODDS ARE ABOUT EVEN

In words with a vowel–consonant–vowel pattern (VCV), the V/CV syllable division occurs just over half the time (55%), and the VC/V syllable division occurs just under half the time (45%).

POP QUIZ

THE LONG AND SHORT OF IT

Read each sentence. Look at the underlined word. Write the word, and divide it into syllables with a slash mark (/). (Hint: Is the first vowel sound long or short?)

1. Tina rode her <u>pony</u> in the contest. _____

2. She hopes to win a gold <u>medal.</u> _____

3. Her pony is named <u>Lady.</u> _____

4. Lady and Tina are in the <u>habit</u> of riding every day. _____

5. They now enter every <u>major</u> competition in the area. _____

6. They compete at the highest <u>level.</u> _____

7. Lady soars <u>over</u> the jumps easily. _____

8. They almost <u>never</u> lose a competition. _____

Answers on page 108.

(Hint: Think two-syllable words!)
Is it better to do your homework on a full or an empty stomach?
Answer: It's better to do it on paper.

HaHA!

What's the hardest part of grammar for criminals?

Ha HA!

Answer: The prison sentence.

The c + le Caboose

Do not fiddle with a poodle in the middle of a puddle!

What do the words *fiddle*, *poodle*, *middle*, and *puddle*
have in common? How do you think you might divide
words like these into syllables?

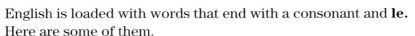 **Rule 4 for dividing words into syllables:** When a
consonant and **le** appear at the end of a word, the final
syllable of the word is the **c + *le*.**

English is loaded with words that end with a consonant and **le.**
Here are some of them.

-ble	-dle	-gle	-tle	-cle	-kle	-ple	-zle
bubble	bridle	angle	battle	circle	ankle	apple	dazzle
double	bundle	bugle	bottle	uncle	crinkle	maple	fizzle
marble	fiddle	eagle	cattle	vehicle	sparkle	purple	muzzle
noble	handle	jungle	gentle		sprinkle	sample	puzzle
pebble	kindle	shingle	kettle		wrinkle	simple	
rumble	middle	single	little			steeple	
stubble	needle	struggle	mantle			temple	
tumble	puddle	wiggle	rattle				
	saddle		settle				
			title				

NOW HERE'S A PICKLE

In words that end in **ckle,** such as *tickle, freckle,* and, of
course, *pickle,* the letters **ck** stand for one sound—the **k**
sound—so they stay together as if they were one consonant.

Syllables Review

If you are having trouble reading or spelling a longer word, try breaking it into syllables. (Remember, each syllable has one vowel sound.) Remember these rules when dividing words into syllables:

✓ **Rule 1:** If a word has two like consonants in the middle, divide between the two consonants.

✓ **Rule 2:** If a word has two unlike consonants in the middle, divide between the two consonants (but *not* if they are a consonant digraph).

✓ **Rule 3:** If a word has a single consonant in the middle, divide before the consonant if the first vowel sound is long and after the consonant if the first vowel sound is short.

✓ **Rule 4:** If a word has a consonant and **le** at the end, divide the word before the consonant.

POP QUIZ

SYLLABLE PARTNERS

Match each syllable in the first column with its **c + le** syllable in the second column. Write the words in the blanks.

un	gle
bub	tle
ti	dle
jun	cle
han	ble
daz	ple
pur	kle
spar	zle

_____

_____

_____

_____

_____

_____

_____

_____

Answers on page 108.

cam el

ANIMAL DIVIDE

Following the rules above, divide each word into syllables with a slash mark (*l*).

camel	hornet	serpent
cattle	monkey	sparrow
chipmunk	parrot	spider
donkey	pony	squirrel
eagle	raccoon	tiger
falcon	rhino	warthog
hippo	robin	zebra

Answers on page 108.

POP QUIZ

POP QUIZ ANSWERS

page 102
How Many Syllables?

shout: 1, late: 1, impossible: 4, wheelbarrow: 3, boy: 1, parade: 2, frown: 1, riddle: 2, responsible: 4, kitchen: 2, sheep: 1, supermarket: 4, deliver: 3, kangaroo: 3, ticket: 2, umbrella: 3, steak: 1, hunger: 2, pepper: 2, necessary: 4, peanut: 2

page 103
Double Divide

pup/pet, fun/ny, jog/ger, mer/ry, hap/py, mir/ror, er/ror, sor/ry, rab/bit, but/ton, mit/ten, cab/bage, buz/zard, sup/pose, of/fice, bliz/zard, bul/let, pep/per, shal/low, com/mon

page 104
Two-Syllable Shuffle

1) trum/pet, 2) nap/kin, 3) in/sect, 4) morn/ing, 5) den/tist, 6) fin/gers, 7) sham/poo, 8) law/yer, 9) par/ty, 10) blan/ket

page 105
The Long and Short of It

1) po/ny, 2) med/al, 3) La/dy, 4) hab/it, 5) ma/jor, 6) lev/el, 7) o/ver, 8) nev/er

page 107
Syllable Partners

uncle, bubble, title, jungle, handle, dazzle, purple, sparkle

page 107
Animal Divide

cam/el, cat/tle, chip/munk, don/key, ea/gle, fal/con, hip/po, hor/net, mon/key, par/rot, po/ny, rac/coon, rhi/no, rob/in, ser/pent, spar/row, spi/der, squir/rel, ti/ger, wart/hog, ze/bra

Prefixes and Suffixes
The Magic of Before and After

Joe thinks the show he just saw was unexciting. Moe thinks it was just plain dull!
Moe obviously doesn't know about the word-building magic of prefixes,
endings, and suffixes!

Once you have learned a new word, you can actually say you have learned several new words. That's because you can use the new word as a base for building other words—simply by adding prefixes, endings, and suffixes. For example, you know the word *color*. You can use *color* to build words such as these:

colored	*colorful*	*discolored*
coloring	*colorless*	*recolored*

These words all have *color* as their main, or base, word, but they have different meanings because of the letters added before and/or after the base word.

Prefix Potions

It's magical. By adding just two letters, you can completely change the meaning of a sentence.

I am so happy.   I am so unhappy.

How is the second sentence different from the first sentence? Look closely. The letters **un** were added to the beginning of *happy*. Two little letters may not seem like much of a change. But these two letters changed the meaning of the word *happy*, and that changed the meaning of the whole sentence.

The letters **un** are a **prefix.** A prefix is a group of letters added to the beginning of a word. When a prefix is added to a base word, it changes the meaning of the base word. (As a matter of fact, **pre-** is a prefix that means *before*.)

PREFIX + BASE WORD = WORD WITH NEW MEANING

A prefix does change the meaning of a base word, but it does not change the spelling of the base word.

mis- + *spell* = *misspell*   **dis-** + *order* = *disorder*

misspell
There's a *miss* in *miss*pell.

POP QUIZ

PREFIX PRACTICE!

There are two parts to this quiz. First, add the prefix to each word and write the new word in the blank. Next, draw a line to match the new word to its synonym. (A synonym is a word that means the same thing.)

un- + like	_____	rough
un- + harmed	_____	still
un- + even	_____	different
un- + real	_____	unlawful
in- + active	_____	safe
in- + credible	_____	lose
il- + legal	_____	imaginary
mis- + place	_____	unbelievable

Answers on page 119.

What does a frog look like when it has a broken leg?
Answer: unhoppy

HaHA!

Why did the orchestra quit?
Answer: It disbanded.

Abracadabra! Endings and Suffixes

You know that adding prefixes to base words makes new words. You can also add **endings** and **suffixes** to base words to make more words. While prefixes are added to the beginning of base words, endings and suffixes are added to the end.

What's the difference between an ending and a suffix? A suffix is like a prefix; it changes the base word's meaning. An ending doesn't change the base word's meaning.

ENDINGS

BASE WORD + ENDING = NEW WORD *(SAME MEANING AS BASE WORD)*

✓ To make singular nouns plural, add the ending **-s** or **-es.**

rabbit + **-s** = *rabbits*   *box* + **-es** = *boxes*

Adding **-s** or **-es** does not change the meanings of the words *rabbit* and *box*.

✓ Add the ending **-s, -es, -ed,** or **-ing** to verbs to show when action is taking place.

-s shows the action happens in the present or happens all the time.
> Anna point**s** at the rabbit.

-ed shows the action happened in the past.
> Anna point**ed** at the rabbit.

-ing shows the action is happening right now and is continuing.
> Anna is point**ing** at the rabbit.

Adding **-s, -ed,** or **-ing** does not change the meaning of the word *point*.

✓ Add the ending **-er** or **-est** to adjectives when the adjectives are being used to make comparisons.

-er is used when two things are being compared.
> That rabbit is small**er** than this rabbit.

-est is used when three or more things are being compared.
> This rabbit is the small**est** of all.

SUFFIXES

BASE WORD + SUFFIX = WORD WITH NEW MEANING

Adding a suffix changes the way a word is used. That is, it changes the word's part of speech.

Some suffixes turn words into adjectives. For instance, adding **-y** to the noun *sleep* creates the adjective *sleepy.* Suffixes that create adjectives include **-y, -ful, -less, -able,** and **-ible.**

> Adam didn't get much *sleep* last night, so he feels *sleepy* this morning.

mnemonic

dependable
A depend*able* worker is *able.*

mnemonic

The suffix **-ly** turns words into adverbs. By adding **-ly** to the adjective *slow,* you make the adverb *slowly.*

> Adam is *slow,* but this morning he is moving more *slowly* than usual.

sincerely
Look for *rely* in since*rely.*

"Y" THE LONG E?

When the letter **y** is a suffix, it stands for the long **e** vowel sound. So it is acting like a vowel. Remember that when you are adding **-y** to the end of a base word.

So now you know that you can create adjectives and adverbs by adding a suffix to a word. It probably won't surprise you to learn that some suffixes turn words into nouns. Such suffixes include **-er, -or, -ness, -ment, -ion, -tion,** and **-ation.** By adding the suffix **-or** to the verb *collect,* you make the noun *collector.*

> Adam is a *collector;* he likes to *collect* books about magic.

mnemonic

argument
He lost an *e* in the argument.

1-2-3 Magic
Magic Made Easy
Mysterious Magic

ENDLESS WISDOM

Each sentence below is a Chinese proverb, or wise saying. Circle the words that have endings or suffixes. Underline each ending or suffix.

Example: Dismantle the bridge (shortly) after (crossing) it.

1. A fall into a ditch makes you wiser.

2. A jade stone is useless before it is processed; a man is worth little until he is educated.

3. The longer the night lasts, the more our dreams will be.

4. A sly rabbit will have three openings to its den.

5. You won't help shoots grow by pulling them up higher.

Answers on page 119.

What word becomes shorter if you add two letters to it?

Answer: short

Ha HA!

Presto Change-o!

Both endings and suffixes are added to the end of base words. Here's something else they have in common: Sometimes they change the base word's spelling. Endings and suffixes cause spelling changes in three ways:

 doubling the final consonant

 changing **y** to **i**

 dropping the silent **e**

Look at what happens to these words when an ending or a suffix is added.

sun + **-y** = *sunny*   *hurry* + **-ed** = *hurried*   *drive* + **-er** = *driver*

DOUBLE OR NOT

When do you double the final consonant before adding an ending or suffix? Should it be *diping* or *dipping?* Here's the scoop!

If the base word has

> - one syllable,
>
> - one short vowel (as in the words *cat, bed, tip, cot,* and *sun*), **and**
>
> - one consonant at the end:

double the final consonant before adding an ending or a suffix <u>that begins with a vowel.</u>

Look at the word *wet. Wet* has one syllable, one short vowel (**e**), and one consonant at the end. So, to add **-er** to *wet,*

$$wet + \textbf{-er} = wetter$$

If you add an ending or a suffix <u>that begins with a consonant,</u> such as **-ness,** don't change the base word.

$$wet + \textbf{-ness} = wetness$$

How about words with more than one syllable? How can you tell when to double the final consonant? It depends on which syllable in the word is **accented,** or said with more stress.

If the base word

> - has two or more syllables,
>
> - is accented on the last syllable, **and**
>
> - has one consonant at the end:

double the final consonant before adding an ending or a suffix <u>that begins with a vowel.</u> If the last syllable is not accented, don't change the spelling.

Suppose you want to add the ending **-ing** to the words *order* and *begin.* Say the words. Which syllable is accented? *Order* is stressed on the beginning syllable, so its spelling does not change. *Begin* is stressed on the last syllable, so double the **n** before adding the ending.

$$order + \textbf{-ing} = ordering \qquad begin + \textbf{-ing} = beginning$$

POP QUIZ

DOUBLE OR NOTHING

Add the endings and suffixes to the base words. Decide whether to double the final consonant or not.

hot + **-er**	_____	hot + **-ness** _____
grin + **-ing**	_____	pain + **-ful** _____
bat + **-ed**	_____	wag + **-ing** _____
forget + **-ing**	_____	forget + **-ful** _____
enter + **-ing**	_____	rub + **-ed** _____
sun + **-y**	_____	fit + **-ing** _____
regret + **-ful**	_____	limit + **-ed** _____
commit + **-ment**	_____	commit + **-ed** _____
wrap + **-ing**	_____	garden + **-er** _____
pot + **-er**	_____	market + **-ing** _____

Answers on page 119.

Why are pilots bad at basketball? (Hint: Think single consonant–plus–ending.)

Answer: They keep traveling.

HaHA!

PUT *Y* IN PLACE OF *I*

OK, so you see that a base word ends with **y.**

What now? You have to look at the letter before the **y.** Is that letter a vowel or a consonant?

✓ When adding an ending or a suffix to a word that ends in a vowel + **y,** keep the **y.**

> *delay* + **-ed** = *delayed*　　　　　　*joy* + **-ful** = *joyful*

✓ When adding an ending or a suffix to a word that ends in a consonant + **y,** you must change the **y** to **i.**

> *reply* + **-ed** = *replied*　　　　　　*busy* + **-ness** = *business*

(When adding **-ing,** however, the **y** stays the same.)

> *reply* + **-ing** = *replying*

ROCK-A-Y BABIES

Combine the words and the endings or suffixes in parentheses ( ). Write the new words in the blanks to finish each sentence. (Remember to change **y** to **i** when necessary.)

"Are the twins _____ (cry + **-ing**)?" asked Mom.

The noise made the _____ (puppy + **-es**) begin to howl.

First, we _____ (try + **-ed**) rocking them.

"Tell them our _____ (funny + **-est**) jokes," said my little

brother. Other _____ (family + **-es**) on the block had their

own ideas. Everyone tried to get the _____ (baby + **-es**)

back to sleep. "Warm milk will make them _____

(sleepy + **-er**)," said Mrs. Gomez. A big family can sometimes be

_____ (try + **-ing**)!

Answers on page 119.

POP QUIZ

(Hint: Think of words that end in y.)

What did the corn do in the band?
Answer: He played by ear.
HaHA!

When did the fly fly?
Answer: When the spider spied it.
Ha HA!

OFF WITH THE *E*

What do the words *make*, *shine*, *rare*, and *grace* have in common? They all end with silent **e**. (Remember, the **e** is silent because it doesn't stand for a vowel sound.) So does anything happen to this **e** when you add an ending or a suffix to the base word? Sometimes yes, sometimes no.

✔ If the ending or suffix begins with a vowel, drop the **e** before adding the ending or suffix.

> *make* + **-ing** = *making*   *shine* + **-y** = *shiny*

✔ If the ending or suffix begins with a consonant, keep the **e** before adding the ending or suffix.

> *rare* + **-ly** = *rarely*   *grace* + **-ful** = *graceful*

POP QUIZ

STRONG SILENT E

Combine each word with the two endings or suffixes.
Write the two new words on the lines.

1. *love*   + **-ly**   _____

        + **-able**   _____

2. *name*   + **-ed**   _____

        + **-less**   _____

3. *close*   + **-ly**   _____

        + **-er**   _____

4. *amaze* + **-ment**   _____

        + **-ing**   _____

5. *use*   + **-ed**   _____

        + **-ful**   _____

Answers on page 119.

Prefixes and Suffixes: Review

This chapter has covered a lot of information about adding prefixes, endings,
and suffixes to base words. These rules will help you build lots of new words—
and become a better speller.

Prefixes

✓ are letters added at the beginning of a base word.

✓ do change the meaning of the base word.

✓ do not change the spelling of the base word.

Endings

✓ are letters added at the end of a base word.

✓ do not change the meaning of the base word.

✓ often change the spelling of the base word.

Suffixes

✓ are letters added at the end of a base word.

✓ often change the spelling of the base word.

POP QUIZ

AWESOME KID INVENTORS

This writer had problems adding prefixes, endings, and suffixes to base words. But now that you know all the rules, it should be a cinch for you! See if you can find all the misspellings. Circle each misspelled word, and write the correct word on a separate piece of paper. (Hint: There are 26 misspelled words.)

Inventionses

Margaret Knight was only 9 when she began workking in a cotton mill. She saw a metal shuttle go fliing out of a loom. It hit and injureed a workor. This was in the 1800s, before it became ilegal for young children to work. Also, workers usualy worked in insafe places. Margaret believeed there must be a way to stop these accidentes. The result was her first invention—a device to hold shuttles in place. But if you think that is Margaret's only invention, you are misstaken. She also inventted a machine for makeing paper bags with square bottomes. These bags are still used for carriing groceryes today.

Becky Schroeder was only 14 when she inventted something special. She wantted to be able to write in the dark. She tryed puting phosphorescent paint (paint that glows without giveing off heat) on paper. When Becky put the glowing paper under her writeing paper, she made an incredable discovery. She could see to write in the dark! Lots of people use this inventtion today. Doctors use it at night to read patients' charts without wakeing them. Astronauts use it when they turn off the electricity so the system can reecharge.

Answers on page 120.

page 110
Prefix Practice!
unlike (different), *unharmed* (safe), *uneven* (rough), *unreal* (imaginary), *inactive* (still), *incredible* (unbelievable), *illegal* (unlawful), *misplace* (lose)

page 113
Endless Wisdom
1) wis<u>er</u>; 2) use<u>less</u>, process<u>ed</u>, educat<u>ed</u>; 3) long<u>er</u>, last<u>s</u>, dream<u>s</u>; 4) open<u>ings</u>;
5) shoot<u>s</u>, pull<u>ing</u>, high<u>er</u>

page 115
Double or Nothing
hotter, grinning, batted, forgetting, entering, sunny, regretful, commitment, wrapping, potter, hotness, painful, wagging, forgetful, rubbed, fitting, limited, committed, gardener, marketing

page 116
Rock-a-*y* Babies
crying, puppies, tried, funniest, families, babies, sleepier, trying

page 117
Strong Silent *e*
1) lovely, lovable; 2) named, nameless; 3) closely, closer; 4) amazement, amazing;
5) used, useful

page 118

Awesome Kid Inventors
Inventions

Margaret Knight was only 9 when she began working in a cotton mill. She saw a metal shuttle go flying out of a loom. It hit and injured a worker. This was in the 1800s, before it became illegal for young children to work. Also, workers usually worked in unsafe places. Margaret believed there must be a way to stop these accidents. The result was her first invention—a device to hold shuttles in place. But if you think that is Margaret's only invention, you are mistaken. She also invented a machine for making paper bags with square bottoms. The bags are still used for carrying groceries today.

Becky Schroeder was only 14 when she invented something special. She wanted to be able to write in the dark. She tried putting phosphorescent paint (paint that glows without giving off heat) on paper. When Becky put the glowing paper under her writing paper, she made an incredible discovery. She could see to write in the dark! Lots of people use Becky's invention today. Doctors use it at night to read patients' charts without waking them. Astronauts use it when they turn off the electricity so the system can recharge.

Using a Dictionary
Good Spellers Fight Back

Do you want to become a better speller? A dictionary can help!
For finding out about words, a dictionary is a great source.

A Writer's Best Friend

As a writer, a dictionary is one of your most important tools. It shows you the correct spelling of words. But it does more than that—it tells how to pronounce words, what they mean, and how to use them. To use a dictionary, you need to understand how it is organized.

FROM A TO Z

All the words in a dictionary are listed in alphabetical order. That is, all the words that begin with **a** are listed first, followed by all the words that begin with **b,** and so on.

GUIDE WORDS

At the top of a dictionary page are two guide words. The first guide word is the first word on the page. The second guide word is the last word on the page. If the word you are looking for comes between these two words alphabetically, then that word is on this page in the dictionary.

WHERE TO FIND IT

Which guide words could you use to find each word in the list below? Write the words under their guide words.

| cry | ceiling | circle | climb |
| chute | clock | cube | census |

climax • close

_____

_____

cedar • central

_____

_____

chunky • circuit

_____

_____

crutch • culture

_____

_____

Answers on page 127.

POP QUIZ

OTHER INFORMATION

Did you know that a dictionary is packed full of useful information? Each entry

✔ shows the word divided into syllables.

✔ shows how to pronounce the word using symbols that stand for sounds. (A key in the dictionary explains the symbols.)

✔ gives the word's part of speech, such as *n.* for noun or *adj.* for adjective.

✔ tells the word's meaning, or its definition.

An entry also may use the word in a sample sentence. It may tell about the word's history and give **synonyms** for the word. (Synonyms are words that have the same or similar meanings.)

Look up a word in the dictionary whenever you are not sure of the word's spelling. Look up a word even if you *think* you know how to spell it. It's always a good idea to double-check!

mnemonic

surprise
Put an **r** on both sides
of the **p**: su*r*p*r*ise!

What happened when the English teacher's dictionary was stolen? HaHA!

Answer: He was at a loss for words.

Finding Information

It's true.... Dictionaries are BIG books. Maybe they make you a little nervous. Well, there's nothing to be nervous about. Just grab a dictionary, grab a friend or study partner if there's someone nearby, and time each other as you take turns looking up the following words: *marmot, prism, curtail, random, acute.* See how quickly each of you can find the words. Record your times. Talk about what you might do to speed up the search process.

WHAT'S THE 4-1-1?

Look up these words in a dictionary, and on a separate sheet of paper, write down the definition of each.

donor   blurt   magnate   trivial   inure

Answers on page 127.

"Spelling Demons": Words that Cause Problems

Spelling demons are what you might call words you have trouble spelling. Some words just seem to cause more problems than others! Try as you might to memorize the correct spelling, these words may always trip you up. These words are your own personal spelling demons.

So what's a writer to do? Well, you could try to memorize how to spell these words. But a better idea is to look up the words in a dictionary. Make using the dictionary a habit. Keep a dictionary nearby when you are writing. Use it often. It's your best weapon in the fight to conquer the spelling demons.

ANOTHER WAY TO TAME YOUR DEMONS

Make a dictionary of your own personal spelling demons. Write the words you have had trouble spelling in a small notebook. You don't need to write down all the information the dictionary includes—just writing down the word (spelled correctly, of course!) is usually enough of a reminder. Or, if you wish, include other information, such as definitions or example sentences. Keep your spelling demon dictionary in a handy place, and refer to it often.

mnemonic

separate
There's *a rat* in sep*arat*e.

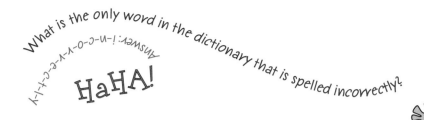

What is the only word in the dictionary that is spelled incorrectly?

Answer: i-n-c-o-r-r-e-c-t-l-y.

HaHA!

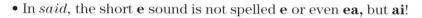

WEIRD BUT WELL-USED WORDS

Some spelling demons are very common words—that have very uncommon spellings! They have sounds that aren't spelled by the letter patterns you have learned. For example:

- In *said*, the short **e** sound is not spelled **e** or even **ea,** but **ai!**

- In *done*, the short **u** sound is not spelled **u** or even **ou,** but **o–e!**

- In *people*, the long **e** sound is not spelled **e, ee, ea, ie,** or even **ei,** but **eo!**

Say these words. Look at the unusual letters that spell the usual sounds.

again	been	does	one	their	to	were
any	buy	of	pull	there	two	what
are	come	once	some	they	was	you

Other, less common words have weird spellings, too. (And *weird* is one of them!) Look at these words. Are these the letters you would expect to spell these sounds?

among	choir	machine	science	answer	column
minute	scissors	broad	friend	quiet	vacuum

mnemonic

friend

I am your fr*i*end.

What happened to the student who swallowed the dictionary?

Answer: The nurse couldn't get a word out of her.

Ha HA!

POP QUIZ

WRITE WEIRD WORDS

Use a word from one of the lists on the previous page to complete each sentence. The more you practice spelling these words, the easier it will be for you to memorize their spelling.

The children wanted to _____ the heavy wagon up the hill. But every time they tried, the wagon rolled down _____. So the children built a special _____ to help them. They used _____ pulleys, one at the top and one at the bottom. It was an idea that the children had learned in _____ class. Once they got started, it took them only a _____ to get that wagon up the hill!

Answers on page 127.

WORDS WITH MISSING SOUNDS

Some words are as difficult to pronounce as they are to spell. When a word is pronounced in some dialects (the way different people pronounce the same word), it becomes even harder to spell correctly. Or sometimes we pronounce the words correctly, but they contain silent letters that don't spell any sounds. Then we try to spell these words the way we say them. Not a good idea! Here are some common mispronunciations that can lead to misspellings.

"libary" for *library*   "artic" for *arctic*   "Febuary" for *February*

Say these words carefully. Look at the way they are spelled. (The tricky parts are printed in bold type.)

bus**i**ness	d**ia**mond	gove**r**nment	rest**au**rant	choc**o**late
family	We**d**nesday	hand**s**ome	su**r**prise	Feb**r**uary
int**e**rested	veg**e**table	diff**er**ent	lis**t**en	

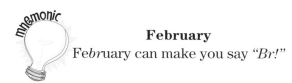

mnemonic

February
Feb**r**uary can make you say *"Br!"*

WHAT'S THE WORD?

Write the word that goes with each clue. Make sure you spell the words correctly.

1. the day before Thursday   _____

2. the month before March   _____

3. what carrots, corn, and potatoes are   _____

4. a building where books are kept   _____

5. not the same   _____

6. something unexpected   _____

Answers on page 127.

SINGLES VS. DOUBLES

Do they or don't they? Whether a word has a single consonant or double consonants is often a tricky question.

access	always	happen	occur	across	banana
harass	until	already	collect	necessary	written

SCHWA: SO WHAT?

As you learned in Chapter 6, the schwa sound can be spelled by any of the five vowel letters **a, e, i, o,** and **u.** In words with the schwa sound, it can be difficult to know which is the correct vowel. (The letters for the schwa sounds in the following words are printed in bold type.)

calend**a**r	s**a**lary	sep**a**rate	dis**e**ase	gramm**a**r	simil**a**r
act**o**r	ben**e**fit	p**u**rsue	par**e**nts	purp**o**se	happ**e**n

WHICH IS RIGHT?

Circle the word in each pair that is spelled correctly. If you're not sure, use a dictionary to help you figure it out.

honor honer   animal animul   survive sirvive

posative positive   organize orginize

Answers on page 127.

page 121

Where to Find It
climax • close: climb, clock; cedar • central: ceiling, census; chunky • circuit: chute, circle; crutch • culture: cry, cube

page 123

What's the 4-1-1?
donor: one that gives, donates, or presents something
blurt: to utter abruptly and impulsively
magnate: a person of rank, power, influence, or distinction often in a specified area
trivial: commonplace, ordinary, of little worth or importance
inure: to accustom to accept something undesirable

page 125

Write Weird Words
pull, again, machine, broad, science, minute

page 126

What's the Word?
1) Wednesday, 2) February, 3) vegetables, 4) library, 5) different, 6) surprise

page 126

Which Is Right?
honor, positive, animal, organize, survive

Index